Success Motivation

SCRIPTURAL SOLUTIONS FOR BEING SUCCESSFUL IN LIFE

Success Motivation

SCRIPTURAL SOLUTIONS FOR BEING SUCCESSFUL IN LIFE

by
Charles Capps

Unless otherwise indicated, all Scripture quotations are taken from the *King James Version* of the Bible.

11 10 09   11 10 9 8 7 6

Success Motivation:
Scriptural Solutions for Being Successful in Life
ISBN 13: 978-0-9820320-8-4
Previously ISBN 10: 1-57794-667-7
Previously ISBN 13: 978-1-57794-667-0
Previously ISBN 0-89274-183-X
Copyright © 1982 by Charles Capps
P.O. Box 69
England, Arkansas 72046

Published by Capps Publishing
PO Box 69
England, AR 72046
Printed in the United States of America.

Contents

Introduction

The power source of life is the Word of God. It is your responsibility to keep your heart with all diligence, for out of it proceed the forces of life. God's Word is truly life to those that find it. He has shared His wisdom with us, and that wisdom is a tree of life to those that lay hold on it.

Many lose their values of life as they climb the ladder of success. God is always interested in your success in life. But He is not interested in your losing health and family to become rich.

God's Word will motivate you to a positive and successful life. When you prosper through God's Word, you are prospering in a way that will work an eternal value in you. The wisdom of God is the Word of God. The Word of God is that tree of life that produces riches, honor, pleasantness, and peace.

There is only one way to achieve true success, and that is through the Word of God. The image that God's Word builds inside you can become the most powerful force in your life. That image will cause you to succeed when others fail.

The teaching in this book is based on principles instead of formulas. Read it carefully.

1

God's Will Is Your Prosperity

Many books have been written on the subject of positive thinking and success, but most of them deal only with the mental realm and lack a spiritual tie-in.

A little power exists in the mental realm and it can change you to some extent; but it takes more than mental assent or a mechanical action for you to prosper abundantly in all areas of your life.

God's Word is spiritual motivation to the human spirit. It will build an image within you and bring you success in every area of your life—financially, spiritually, physically, and socially. These spiritual truths from the Word of God can change your life.

Diligence in God's System

God said through His prophet Hosea, *My people are destroyed for lack of knowledge* (Hos. 4:6). In Luke 16:8, Jesus said, *The children of this world are in their generation wiser than the children of light.* This is true, but it ought not be. The children of the world should not be wiser than the children of light!

The children of the world have been diligent to find out how the world's system operates. Then they operate the system.

The world's system is plain: "Grab and hold! Whatever you get, keep! Work day and night. Seek for riches. Give yourself totally to your work."

God's system is exactly opposite. *Give, and it shall be given* (Luke 6:38).

...he which soweth bountifully shall reap also bountifully (2 Cor. 9:6). *My God shall supply all your need according to his riches in glory by Christ Jesus* (Phil. 4:19).

...godliness is profitable unto all things, having promise of the life that now is, and of that which is to come (1 Tim. 4:8).

Godly men and women *can and will prosper* as they become diligent in God's system. If you have been obedient to give, then you should be expecting to receive a better job, a raise, or new direction in business.

Down through the years, many Christians have somehow decided that it is not God's will for them to prosper on earth. They all believe it will be wonderful when they get to heaven. But we must deal with the "here and now." God's Word gives us the wisdom for prosperity.

To be truly motivated to success, we first must *know that it is God's will for us to prosper!*

Your Soul Must Prosper

God told Adam to have dominion over the earth. From the beginning it was God's intention for man to prosper. Third John 2 says, *Beloved, I wish above all things that thou mayest prosper and be in health, even as thy soul prospereth.*

The word *wish* in this verse in the literal Greek can be translated "pray," so we could read it this way: *Beloved, I* (pray) *above all things that thou mayest prosper and be in health, even as thy soul prospereth.*

One of the problems in the Body of Christ is that their souls are not prospering. The soul of man is the inner link that connects the spirit with the body. The soul and the spirit of man are not the same, though for years many thought they were. The Bible divides the two.

So often we hear this statement: "He has lost his soul." We think of the soul as being the spirit, but the Scriptures tell us differently.

Man is a spirit; he has a soul; and he lives in a body. The soul of man is composed of the mind, the will, and the emotions. It is the guidance system for the *natural* man.

Man is a spirit being, having been breathed out of God. In the beginning, God breathed His spirit life into Adam. That spirit life became the human spirit which operates beyond the intellect in the higher realm—the spiritual realm. The gifts of the Spirit come out of the spiritual realm.

The spirit of a man can receive revelation before his intellect becomes involved. Quite often, I have known something in my spirit, but was unable to put it into words. It was real and strong in my spirit *before* my intellect could grasp it. Some of the things I am sharing in this book became a reality in my spirit several years ago; but it took time for that to be transferred from my spirit to my intellect in order for me to be able to share it with others.

The Apostle John received many things by revelation into his spirit. He wrote, *Ye are of God, little children, and have overcome them: because greater is he that is in you, than he that is in the world* (1 John 4:4).

He didn't say, "Maybe you'll overcome one of these days." He said, "You have *already* overcome because the Greater One is inside you!" This revelation was transferred from God's Spirit to John's human spirit.

John said you should prosper, even as your soul prospers. Your soul must embrace prosperity. *A prosperous soul will produce a prosperous image inside you.*

In the fifth chapter of John's Gospel, Jesus approached a crippled man at the pool of Bethesda and said to him, *Wilt thou be made whole?* (v. 6).

That seems a strange thing to say to a man who is crippled. The man had been lying there for years waiting for the "troubling of the water" so he could go down into the water and be healed. He wanted to be healed, but Jesus asked him, "Will you be made whole?"

The first thing the man did was to begin talking about his problem: *Sir, I have no man, when the water is troubled, to put me into the pool: but while I am coming, another steppeth down before me* (v. 7).

Jesus was trying to get him to speak his faith, but the man zeroed in on the problem instead.

A Desire To Prosper

Do you have a will to prosper? Before you can obtain true prosperity, there must be a desire within you.

Proverbs 13:12 says, *When desire cometh, it is a tree of life.* This verse can be interpreted two ways:

1. When the thing you desire comes, it is the tree of life.

2. When desire is in you, it is a tree of life.

I believe the second is the correct interpretation. In other words, the thing you desire is the thing you will pray and the thing you will say. You will speak in line with your desire and faith comes by hearing. (Rom. 10:17.)

Jesus said, *What things soever ye desire, when ye pray, believe that ye receive them, and ye shall have them* (Mark 11:24). He said believe you receive the things you *desire,* not the things you already have.

If your soul is not prospering, you will have a bad image—an image of failure and defeat or sickness.

Several years ago, I was having problems both financially and physically. Because I had an image of failure inside me, I saw everything I did as a failure. I often said, "It doesn't make any difference what I do. Nothing will work out anyway." I was disgusted with life because of a bad business deal.

I had "put out a fleece" before God as Gideon had done. It worked for Gideon; but when I did it, I really got fleeced!

Jesus said when He went away, He would send another Comforter to *teach you all things* (John 14:26), *guide you into all truth...and...shew you things to come* (John 16:13).

We don't have to use fleeces today. The Spirit of Truth abiding in us will teach us.

When the desire to prosper comes from God's Word, it is truly a tree of life. Then God's Spirit reveals direction. *The preparations of the heart in man, and the answer of the tongue, is from the Lord* (Prov. 16:1).

Religious Tradition—Enemy of Success

A friend of mine, Gary Garner, was with me in a church in Canton, Ohio, a few years ago. I had him give a short testimony. Gary told how he and his wife had been believing God for new furniture for their home.

He said, "We believed it so strongly that we just gave away all our furniture!" Then he explained: "I'm not saying you should do that because, in a sense, we were like Peter: We jumped out of the boat before we were ready! So we sat on the floor for three months!"

When people came to visit, they had to sit on the floor, too! Gary said he appreciated his friends because they didn't feel sorry for "poor Gary" and buy furniture to give him. They let him believe his way out of it. Finally, the money came in and they got new furniture.

After the meeting, a fellow came up to Gary and said, "Brother, you know, I've got old, ragged furniture, too."

Gary grabbed his hand and started to pray, "Father, in the name of Jesus, I pray that You'll prosper this brother and that he'll receive new furniture."

At this, the man said, "No! No!" He jerked his hand away and backed off. "I don't want new furniture. I just came to tell you that you should have been satisfied with what you had!"

"You're too late," Gary said. "I've already got my new furniture, and it's a lot better than the old."

Somehow through the years, people have gotten the idea that you can't serve God and prosper. Several years ago I picked up some of that tradition myself. I thought prosperity was for some people; but every time a trouble, trial, or financial problem came along, I thought it was God trying to teach me something!

I was learning many things, but I wasn't getting anywhere because what I learned was wrong. I finally realized that it wasn't God at all, but the Devil stealing my finances. Then I had to unlearn some things.

I found that God's Word was contrary to my thoughts, contrary to many things I had been taught. I used to think, *Surely, if these principles of faith were true, they would have taught them in my church.* But they didn't know anything about them in that church!

When I started applying these principles by speaking God's Word, things started changing for the better. Results didn't come overnight, but an image began to build inside me.

Second Timothy 3:16-17 says, *All scripture is given by inspiration of God, and is profitable for doctrine, for reproof, for correction, for instruction in righteousness: that the man of God may be perfect, thoroughly furnished unto all good works.*

All Scripture is given by God and is *profitable for us.* Instruction in God's Word will change our preconceived ideas and will teach us to understand prosperity God's way.

Things To Remember

Know God wants you to prosper.

***

Desire to prosper.

***

Use God's system.

***

Speak God's Word.

***

See yourself prospering.

2

God's Willingness on Your Behalf

Second Peter 1:1 gives us an important key to God's willingness toward us. It says:

Simon Peter, a servant and an apostle of Jesus Christ, to them that have obtained like precious faith with us through the righteousness of God and our Saviour Jesus Christ.

Notice who Peter is writing to: *To those that have obtained like precious faith with them.* He is talking to us because we have obtained the same faith.

Grace and peace be multiplied unto you through the knowledge of God, and of Jesus our Lord (v. 2). There is a knowledge of God that will enable God's grace to be *multiplied* to you. Grace has been defined as unmerited favor, but grace is much more than that. Not only is it unmerited favor, it is God's willingness to use His power and ability on your behalf.

It was because God was willing to get personally involved to provide salvation that I was saved.

God's willingness to use His power and ability on our behalf and His peace are multiplied to us *through the knowledge of God.* The word *peace* literally means prosperity. It means "to be joined together as one." If we are joined with Jesus, that's prosperity any way you look at it!

God is not just willing. *His willingness is multiplied to us.* Some say, "I know God is able, but I don't know whether or not He's willing." *He won't until you find out He will.*

You must have the knowledge of God's willingness to prosper you. In the first chapter of Mark, a leper came to Jesus and said, *If thou wilt, thou canst make me clean.* Jesus then stretched forth His hand and laid it on the leper. No healing power flowed until Jesus said, *I will; be thou clean. As soon as he had spoken, immediately the leprosy departed, and he was cleansed* (vv. 40-42).

The leper knew Jesus *could* heal him; but he didn't know whether or not He *would* heal him. Jesus, anointed with the Holy Spirit, laid His hand on the leper, but no healing came until He answered the man's question. No prosperity will come until you answer the poverty question: "Does God want me poor?"

When you know God *will,* then He is willing. If you are in doubt about His willingness, He *won't.* God's willingness and prosperity are multiplied to you through the knowledge of God. As you gain the knowledge of God, you will have faith in that knowledge, and it will multiply God's willingness toward you.

Prosperity in All Areas

It is possible for prosperity to be limited to only one area of your life. People who are diligent in certain areas will prosper in those areas.

Some denominations are diligent in presenting salvation; they are successful in that area. Others, who are successful in the area of healing and walking in divine health, fail when it comes to finances.

Many don't understand why this happens. In trying to answer these questions, some have said, "Well, it must not be God's will for me to be prosperous or healed."

We could spend all our time dealing with divine healing and get people healed; but if we did, not many would prosper financially. We must find a balance.

Romans 4:3 says, *Abraham believed God, and it was counted unto him for righteousness.* The word *righteousness* is an Old English word that means "right standing with God." Abraham was in right standing with God.

It is possible for an individual to be in right standing with God in the area of salvation, but not be in right standing on healing or finances. He may be thinking and believing wrong. His preconceived ideas may be contrary to Scripture.

A person who is in right standing with the Scriptures on healing will usually get healed, but that same person may be out of right standing concerning finances. He might believe that it's a sin to have money or drive a new car. He could be right in his heart, but wrong in his head.

In the soulish area he can be wrong. If his soul is not prosperous in that particular area, then usually he will not prosper in that area. A person in this condition will not give much into the ministry because he doesn't believe God wants him to have anything. Therefore, he never believes for a return, and if it comes, he misses it. It takes a prosperous attitude to reap a financial harvest.

God's Word says, *Whatsoever he doeth shall prosper* (Ps. 1:3). You can apply this verse to supply even small needs. For instance, I have used it even on fishing trips. A few years ago I was fishing with two fellows. One kept saying, "There aren't any fish left here. We caught them all out of here two years ago!"

Having had enough of that negative talk, I grabbed my rod and reel, jumped out of the boat, and waded away from the unbelief.

I started saying, "Whatever I do will prosper, in the name of Jesus! No weapon formed against me will prosper!" (I knew that supper would be slim if we didn't catch some fish!)

Before long, I caught a five-pound bass. One of the fellows asked, "What did you catch him on?" I yelled back, "Psalm 1:3!" I have filled a stringer many times with that verse.

It's time for Christians to get a healthy attitude toward prosperity in *every* area! God even wants you to prosper in the little things.

Jesus Became Poor That You Might Be Rich

For ye know the grace of our Lord Jesus Christ, that, though he was rich, yet for your sakes he became poor, that ye through his poverty might be rich (2 Cor. 8:9).

Jesus suffered the curse of the Law: poverty, sickness, and spiritual death. When He was here on earth, He was poverty-stricken according to the world's system. He didn't have a house or a place to lay His head. Yet all His needs were met because He operated according to spiritual law.

He became poor ...*that ye through his poverty might be rich*. Someone has suggested that this was talking about Jesus being poor spiritually. How poor was Christ spiritually? He raised the dead, cast out demons, healed the sick. No, He was not poverty-stricken spiritually in His ministry.

Jesus became poor so that you might be rich—but He's not poor anymore!

Everything He did was for us. His poverty brought us access to prosperity.

Joint-heirs With the King

Romans 8:17 tells us we are joint-heirs with Jesus Christ. That means whatever He has, we have access to through the Word of God.

Jesus said, *When he, the Spirit of truth, is come, he will guide you into all truth ...All things that the Father hath are mine: therefore said I, that he shall take of mine, and shall shew it unto you* (John 16:13,15).

We must realize that God is not poor and that we are redeemed from the curse of poverty. God *wants* us to walk in victory—spiritually, physically, financially, and socially.

Ask According to God's Will

Jesus made the following statement several times in His ministry: *Ask, and it shall be given you; seek, and ye shall find; knock, and it shall be opened unto you* (Matt. 7:7).

Someone may say, "That can't be true, because I asked and didn't receive."

Statements like Matthew 7:7 must be qualified. You must ask in faith. If you apply the principles of God's Word, then you will know the will and purpose of God. As a result, faith will come; then when you ask, you will receive.

Jesus said in John 15:7, *If ye abide in me, and my words abide in you, ye shall ask what ye will, and it shall be done unto you.*

Someone may say, "If this statement was true, everyone would be a millionaire." No, there is more to it than that. Jesus didn't just say, "If ye abide in Me, ask what you will." He included a qualification: "If ye abide in Me, *and My words abide in you,* ask what ye will." God's Word is His will, and God's will is His Word. When His Word abides in you, then His will abides in you.

God sent his word, and healed them (Ps. 107:20). *They* [God's words] *are life unto those that find them, and health (medicine) to all their flesh* (Prov. 4:22).

It is God's will to heal you in every way you can believe—spiritually, physically, and financially. God's Word will work to that end, if you will learn to apply it wisely.

Saying and Believing

The Word of God tells us to speak what we desire. In Mark 11:23-24 Jesus gives the foundation principles for the God kind of faith:

Whosoever shall say unto this mountain, Be thou removed, and be thou cast into the sea; and shall not doubt in his heart, but shall believe that those things which he saith shall come to pass; he shall have whatsoever he saith.

Therefore I say unto you, What things soever ye desire, when ye pray, believe that ye receive them, and ye shall have them.

In this passage of Scripture, the word *therefore* connects the two verses. Jesus is saying, "When a man believes and doubts not in his heart, he will have what he is saying; *therefore,* he will receive what he desires when he prays."

When you pray, believe you receive what you desire! In other words, pray the desire, not the problem!

When I first read this verse, I thought it worked for *whosoever;* but Jesus didn't say that. He said it would work for *whosoever shall say.* Saying that the principle works for *whosoever* is like saying, "Farming will work for anybody." Farming works only for those who plant seed.

To operate the principle of Mark 11:23, you must plant the seed; and to do this, you must get your mouth in motion! You won't receive your desire just because you say it. You will receive it because of the way the Kingdom of God operates. Saying it is involved in working the principle.

Believe and Don't Doubt

Besides *saying,* this principle says the *whosoever* must *believe* and *doubt not* in his heart.

Speak your desire, then meditate on it. Keep it in your mouth. This will put it in your heart; then faith will come and what you desired will eventually come to you.

Whosoever believes *those things which he saith* shall come to pass. Notice he believes everything he says will come to pass; and because of that, *he shall have whatsoever he saith.* If you say the wrong things—words of doubt and unbelief—you are on your way to trouble because you are sowing the wrong seed.

Wrong seed will bring a wrong harvest. These are Kingdom principles; and to operate in the principles of the Kingdom, we must have the wisdom of God. *The Lord giveth wisdom: out of his mouth cometh knowledge and understanding* (Prov. 2:6).

Things To Remember

God is willing to use His power and ability on your behalf.

Know that God wants you to prosper in *all* areas.

Prosperity requires diligence.

It takes a prosperous attitude to reap a financial harvest.

Jesus became poor that you might be rich.

His poverty brings you access to prosperity.

God wants you to walk in victory—
spiritually, physically, financially, and socially.

Pray your desire, not your problem.

Meditate on and speak your desire.

3

God's Wisdom Is Available to You

My son, if thou wilt receive my words, and hide my commandments with thee; so that thou incline thine ear unto wisdom, and apply thine heart to understanding;

Yea, if thou criest after knowledge, and liftest up thy voice for understanding; if thou seekest her as silver, and searchest for her as for hid treasures;

Then shalt thou understand the fear of the Lord, and find the knowledge of God.

Proverbs 2:1-5

God's Wisdom: More Valuable Than Gold

If someone told you that gold nuggets and diamonds had been found on your property, you would be diligent to sift through the dirt, searching for that treasure!

The Word of God is worth more to you than all the gold and diamonds in the world. But many never turn the pages for its riches. *The Lord giveth wisdom: out of his mouth cometh knowledge and understanding* (Prov. 2:6). Wisdom comes out of the mouth of God: Wisdom is the Word of God!

He layeth up sound wisdom for the righteous; he is a buckler to them that walk uprightly.

He keepeth the paths of judgment, and preserveth the way of saints.

Then shalt thou understand righteousness, and judgment, and equity; yea, every good path.

Proverbs 2:7-9

If you follow the wisdom of God, you will understand every good path.

God Wants You To Have His Wisdom

Wisdom crieth without; she uttereth her voice in the streets: she crieth in the chief place of concourse, in the openings of the gates: in the city she uttereth her words, saying,

How long, ye simple ones, will ye love simplicity? and the scorners delight in their scorning, and fools hate knowledge?

Behold, I will pour out my spirit unto you, I will make known my words unto you.

Proverbs 1:20-23

When wisdom entereth into thine heart, and knowledge— the knowledge that God wants you prosperous in every area of your life—*is pleasant unto thy soul...* (Prov. 2:10), **then:**

Discretion shall preserve thee, understanding shall keep thee:

To deliver thee from the way of the evil man, from the man that speaketh froward things.

Proverbs 2:11,12

Wisdom Brings Success

God wants you to have wisdom so that you will be blessed and prosperous:

Happy is the man that findeth wisdom, and the man that getteth understanding. For the merchandise of it is better than the merchandise of silver, and the gain thereof than fine gold.

She is more precious than rubies: and all the things thou canst desire are not to be compared unto her. Length of days is in her right hand; and in her left hand riches and honour.

Proverbs 3:13-16

How does wisdom get into your heart? It comes from the mouth of God! Then you must believe it and speak it out your mouth. David said, *My tongue is the pen of a ready writer* (Ps. 45:1).

Things To Remember

Wisdom comes out of the mouth of God.

God wants you to have wisdom so you will be blessed and prosperous.

You get wisdom into your heart by believing God's Word and speaking it out your mouth.

4

Knowledge of the Kingdom

God always intended for His Kingdom to be on earth. You will not spend eternity in heaven but on earth—the new earth.

God created Adam to be god over the earth, to rule it. Man was subordinate to God, but he was to have dominion over the earth.

God told Adam how to prosper. He said, ...*replenish the earth, and subdue it: and have dominion over every living thing that moveth upon the earth* (Gen. 1:28). God gave that authority to Adam, with only one stipulation: *of the tree of the knowledge of good and evil, thou shalt not eat...* (Gen. 2:17).

God's will was that the earth be patterned after heaven. After turning the earth over to Adam, God let Adam do as he chose. When Adam was about to sin by disobeying God, God didn't say, "No, Adam, you can't do that." He had given Adam total authority. When Adam sold out to Satan by eating the forbidden fruit the serpent (Satan) offered, God did not lift a finger to stop him. Why? Because it was not God's responsibility to do so; it was Adam's responsibility.

Someone has suggested that Adam was nothing more than a weed puller in the Garden. But he couldn't have been—there were no weeds in the Garden.

Adam was god over the earth. In 2 Corinthians 4:4, Paul refers to Satan as *the god of this world who has blinded the minds of them which believe not.* Satan got this title from Adam.

God Establishes His Kingdom

After Adam sinned and allowed Satan to become god of the world, God used another means to restore His Kingdom to earth: He established a blood covenant with Abraham. The Covenant meant that whatever Abraham had belonged to God and whatever God had belonged to Abraham. That's how strong their blood covenant was.

As you study this Covenant, you will find that Abraham was exceedingly rich because God made him rich.

> *When Abram was ninety years old and nine, the Lord appeared to Abram, and said unto him, I am the Almighty God; walk before me, and be thou perfect. And I will make my covenant between me and thee, and will multiply thee exceedingly. And Abram fell on his face: and God talked with him.*
>
> Genesis 17:1-3

God said to Abraham, "I am *El Shaddai* (Almighty God)." In the Hebrew, the word *almighty* or *El Shaddai* means "the all-sufficient One, the God Who is more than enough."

Some seem to think that God said, "I am El Cheapo." To them God and poverty run hand in hand. But that's not true! You read in the book of Revelation that the streets of heaven are pure gold. There are even gates in heaven made out of a single pearl! (Rev. 21:21.)

God told Abraham that He would make him the father of many nations:

> *Neither shall thy name any more be called Abram, but thy name shall be Abraham; for a father of many nations have I made thee.*
>
> *And I will establish my covenant between me and thee and thy seed after thee in their generations for an everlasting covenant, to be a God unto thee, and to thy seed after thee.*
>
> Genesis 17:5,7

We can see from the blessings of the Covenant described in the following scriptures that God didn't intend for Abraham or his descendants to be poverty-stricken. The promise was to Abraham and his seed in their generation.

> *It shall come to pass, if thou shalt hearken diligently unto the voice of the Lord thy God, to observe and to do all his commandments which I command thee this day, that the Lord thy God will set thee on high above all nations of the earth:*
>
> *And all these blessings shall come on thee, and overtake thee, if thou shalt hearken unto the voice of the Lord thy God.*
>
> *Blessed shalt thou be in the city, and blessed shalt thou be in the field....Blessed shall be thy basket and thy store.*
>
> *Blessed shalt thou be when thou comest in, and blessed shalt thou be when thou goest out.*
>
> Deuteronomy 28:1-3,5,6

Conditional Promises

> *And the Lord shall make thee the head, and not the tail; and thou shalt be above only, and thou shalt not be beneath; if that thou hearken unto the commandments of the Lord*

thy God, which I command thee this day, to observe and to do them.

Deuteronomy 28:13

It shall come to pass, if thou shalt hearken diligently unto the voice of the Lord thy God all these blessings shall come on thee...and overtake thee.

Deuteronomy 28:1,2

This last scripture says we are to *hearken diligently* to God's Word. The word *hearken* means "to hear intelligently, be obedient to, declare and tell." The word *diligently* means "to declare wholly and completely, louder and louder." So let's read it with that meaning:

If thou shalt hearken diligently unto the voice of the Lord thy God—to hear intelligently, be obedient to, and declare or speak louder and louder what God has said—then *all these blessings shall come on thee.*

God said to speak out His Word; but from the way some people talk, you would think He said to declare all the curses, to talk about how it won't work and how it failed the last time it was tried.

Choose Blessings, Not Curses

And it shall be, if thou do at all forget the Lord thy God, and walk after other gods, and serve them, and worship them, I testify against you this day that ye shall surely perish.

As the nations which the Lord destroyeth before your face, so shall ye perish; because ye would not be obedient unto the voice of the Lord your God.

Deuteronomy 8:19,20

God is warning of the consequences of disobeying His voice and of the curses that would come upon the people who forsook the Lord and served other gods.

In Deuteronomy, chapter 28, God describes the curse of poverty:

> *Because thou servedst not the Lord thy God with joyfulness, and with gladness of heart, for the **abundance of all things;***
>
> *Therefore shalt thou serve thine enemies which the Lord shall send against thee, in hunger, and in thirst, and in nakedness, and in want of all things: and he shall put a yoke of iron upon thy neck, until he have destroyed thee.*
>
> vv. 47,48

God was encouraging the children of Israel to be obedient to the Word; but they failed to be obedient and the curses did come on them.

The Covenant of Blessing applies to the seed of Abraham in the same way it applied to the children of Israel. The blessings will overtake us if we hearken diligently to God's voice.

God said to Abraham, *I will make my covenant between me and thee, and will multiply thee exceedingly.... As for me, behold, my covenant is with thee* (Gen. 17:2,4).

Paul says the promise was that Abraham should be heir of the world. (Rom. 4:13.)

The Covenant Reestablishes the Kingdom

When Adam committed high treason against God, allowing Satan to become the god of this world, a curse of poverty, sickness, and spiritual death came upon the land. (Gen. 3:17,18.) God established the Covenant to relieve His people from this curse.

In Deuteronomy 28:15, God said, *But it shall come to pass, if thou wilt not hearken unto the voice of the Lord thy God, to observe to do all his commandments and his statutes which I command thee this day; that all these curses shall come upon thee, and overtake thee....* Then He listed the curses.

After reading this scripture, some people form a bad image of God, believing that He does evil things. But God was warning His people. He was telling them what would happen if they got over among the curses. He was saying that the curses existed, but that the people didn't have to let the curses affect them.

Abraham's Blessings Are Ours!

In Genesis 17:7, God said, *I will establish my covenant between me and thee and thy seed after thee in their generations for an everlasting covenant, to be a God unto thee, and to thy seed after thee.*

Abraham and his descendants through Isaac were to operate in the Covenant until that Seed came.

Let's take a closer look at the seed: *Now to Abraham and his seed were the promises made. He saith not, And to seeds, as of many; but as of one...* (Gal. 3:16).

What "seed" is this talking about?

...And to thy seed, which is Christ.

We are all the children of God and the seed of Abraham. Galatians 3:26-29 makes this very plain:

For ye are all the children of God by faith in Christ Jesus.

For as many of you as have been baptized into Christ have put on Christ.

There is neither Jew nor Greek, there is neither bond nor free, there is neither male nor female: for ye are all one in Christ Jesus. And if ye be Christ's, then are ye Abraham's seed, and heirs according to the promise.

Paul says, *Now ye are the body of Christ* (1 Cor. 12:27). When we are born again, we are baptized into Christ. Christ is the seed; and since we are part of the Body of Christ, we are the seed. Therefore, the promise God made to Abraham belongs to us today.

For if the inheritance be of the law, it is no more of promise: but God gave it to Abraham by promise.

Wherefore then serveth the law? It was added because of transgressions, till the seed should come to whom the promise was made; and it was ordained by angels in the hand of a mediator...

But before faith came, we were kept under the law, shut up unto the faith which should afterwards be revealed.

Wherefore the law was our schoolmaster to bring us unto Christ, that we might be justified by faith.

But after that faith is come, we are no longer under a schoolmaster.

Galatians 3:18,19,23-26

We are no longer under the Law. That means we are no longer under the curse of the Law. Glory to God, Christ redeemed us from the curse, not the blessing—the blessing is still ours!

Christ hath redeemed us from the curse of the law, being made a curse for us: for it is written, Cursed is every one that hangeth on a tree:

That the blessing of Abraham might come on the Gentiles through Jesus Christ; that we might receive the promise of the Spirit through faith.

Galatians 3:13,14

Many believe that the promise of the Spirit is God's promise to send the Holy Spirit; but it is the promise of the Spirit to Abraham in regard to the Covenant. God was saying that because Christ redeemed us from the curse of the Law, then the blessings of Abraham belong to us.

The Covenant Is Everlasting

Brethren, I speak after the manner of men; Though it be but a man's covenant, yet if it be confirmed, no man disannulleth, or addeth thereto...

And this I say, that the covenant, that was confirmed before of God in Christ, the law, which was four hundred and thirty years after, cannot disannul, that it should make the promise of none effect.

Galatians 3:15,17

The Law came into effect after God had made the Covenant with Abraham. While under the Law and under the curse of it, the Israelites were sold into slavery in Egypt and had to stay there all those years. But God said the Law still could not disannul the Covenant because His was an everlasting Covenant.

In this Covenant which God said He would establish with Abraham's seed, there is the phrase *in their generations.* That means all the way down! It is an everlasting Covenant. It will continue to the end of the ages. A blood covenant was so binding that even unborn children were involved until they could decide for themselves whether or not they would come under that covenant.

Every believer who wants to come into that Covenant today can claim it and walk in the benefits of it just like Abraham did! In fact, they can walk in it better than Abraham for he was under the Old Covenant. The New Covenant is established on better promises.

If the Old Covenant had been perfect, there would have been no need for a new covenant; but finding fault, God made a new covenant—one that was signed and sealed by Jesus with His own blood. Notice this covenant was everlasting. It did not pass away with the Old Covenant being fulfilled.

Place Yourself Under This Covenant

When I saw the truth in Genesis 17:7—that we are entitled to be in that Covenant—I decided to place myself under the Covenant. I spoke this out loud:

"In the name of Almighty God and His Son, Jesus Christ, I decide now to come under that Covenant! I'm going to operate in it! I open myself now, Father, to let You establish it with me in my generation!"

Make a decision to come under that Covenant and walk in it. You have a covenant with God. *But thou shalt remember the Lord thy God: for it is he that giveth thee power to get wealth, that he may establish his covenant which he sware unto thy fathers, as it is this day* (Deut. 8:18).

Things To Remember

God created man to have dominion over the earth.

Adam's sin allowed Satan to become the god of the world.

God established a blood covenant with Abraham.

Everything Abraham had belonged to God.

Everything God had belonged to Abraham.

Hearken diligently to the voice of God's Word.

*If ye be Christ's, then are ye Abraham's seed,
and heirs according to the promise.*

Place yourself under this Covenant.
Make the decision to walk with God.

You have an everlasting Covenant with Him!

5

The Kingdom Has Come

In the sixth chapter of Matthew, Jesus is teaching His disciples how to pray:

After this manner therefore pray ye: Our Father which art in heaven, hallowed be thy name. Thy kingdom come. Thy will be done in earth, as it is in heaven (vv. 9,10).

This prayer, which we know today as *The Lord's Prayer,* is not a New Testament prayer; it is an Old Testament prayer.

Sometimes people point to *The Lord's Prayer* and say, "Here's the way Jesus taught us to pray."

No, this is not the way Jesus taught us to pray. He taught His disciples to pray under the Old Covenant. Sometimes people don't realize that even though the four Gospels—Matthew, Mark, Luke, and John—are in the New Testament, the people were still operating under the Law. They were living in a transition period between the Old and New Covenants.

"Thy Kingdom Come"

I want you to notice Jesus' words: *Thy kingdom come.* In other words, He was saying, "Pray that the Kingdom of God would come, that the will of God would be done in earth as it is in heaven."

The earth was designed to be a duplicate of heaven, to operate in the same way as heaven. The will of God is for it to be the same on earth as it is in heaven.

Someone might say, "But it's not that way. Earth isn't like heaven."

No, it's not that way. Jesus knew it wasn't that way; but He said, "Pray that it will get that way." Jesus would not have taught us to pray against the will of God. The will of God under the Old Covenant was for earth to be the same as heaven.

As we saw in Chapter 2, God's intention from the beginning was for His Kingdom to be on earth, and He has not changed. If Adam had been obedient to what God told him to do, it would have been that way today. But Adam committed high treason and turned his authority over to the Devil. When he did, the forces of evil were loosed upon earth.

God's will is still the same today as it was in the beginning—and it will be performed in the end! When the earth is renovated, it will be the way God intended it to be—heaven on earth.

"Some Shall See the Kingdom"

For the Son of man shall come in the glory of his Father with his angels; and then he shall reward every man according to his works.

Verily I say unto you, There be some standing here, which shall not taste of death, till they see the Son of man coming in his kingdom.

Matthew 16:27,28

Evidently, Jesus is talking of two different things. In verse 27, He is talking about His return to earth and the reward that will be given. Then in verse 28, He says that some of those standing with Him would not taste of death until they saw Him coming in His Kingdom. That was nearly two thousand years ago! How could those men not taste death until Jesus returned in His Kingdom?

When Jesus said, *There be some standing here, which shall not taste of death, till they see the Son of man coming in his kingdom,* He was not referring to the literal Kingdom of God which is going to be set up here on earth after His return. This statement would surely prove that Jesus was talking about the Kingdom of God that is within man.

When Jesus was raised from the dead, He came forth as the glorified Son of God. He carried His blood into the heavenlies and made atonement for man, setting in motion the New Covenant.

As the risen Christ, He appeared to His disciples many times. One time, according to John 20:22, He breathed on them and said, *Receive ye the Holy Ghost.*

I believe this is symbolic of what happened on the day of Pentecost. (Acts 2:1-4.) They were all in one accord in one place; and there came a sound of a rushing, mighty wind that filled all the place where they were sitting. On that day, Jesus came to dwell in the hearts of men in the Person of the Holy Spirit. The Kingdom of God truly had come to earth!

During His earthly ministry, Jesus, the Son of God, met all the needs of the people in that day: He healed the sick, raised the dead, cast out demons, and on two occasions fed the multitudes with only a few loaves and fish.

After doing all these things, He said to them, *It is expedient for you that I go away* (John 16:7). In other words, "You would be better off if I go away."

I am sure they thought, *How would we be better off if He goes away?*

Then He said, *If I go not away, the Comforter* [the Holy Ghost] *will not come unto you.* In that day, Jesus was able to minister only to the people He came into contact with. Limited by His physical body, He could be in only one place at a time. So it was better for Him to go away and send the Holy Spirit. Once He had come in the Person of the Holy Spirit, His power would be limitless.

The Godhead Dwells in You

In John 14:23 He said, *If a man love me, he will keep my words: and my Father will love him, and we will come unto him, and make our abode with him.* In other words, Jesus was promising that the whole Godhead—the Father, the Son, and the Holy Ghost—would dwell in us.

> *When he was demanded of the Pharisees, when the kingdom of God should come, he answered them and said, The kingdom of God cometh not with observation:*
>
> *Neither shall they say, Lo here! Or, lo there! for, behold, the kingdom of God is within you.*
>
> Luke 17:21

The above passage clearly shows that when Jesus told His disciples in Matthew 6:10 to pray *Thy kingdom come,* He was talking about the inward establishment of the Kingdom of God, not the physical kingdom that will be set up at the end of the ages.

Again we can apply the law of double reference. Jesus said, "Pray that the will of God be done in the earth the same way it is in heaven." The physical body of man was made out of the dust of the earth; the inner man was not. The real creation was breathed out of the mouth of God, the Spirit of God. Adam was created to fellowship with Diety. God is a spirit. Spirits don't communicate with bodies. The communication God had with Adam in the Garden was in the spirit realm. The real you is the human spirit.

Jesus said to pray that the will of God be done in the earth as it is in heaven.

We don't have to pray *Thy kingdom come* today because it has already come! If you have been born again, the Kingdom is within you. The Kingdom abides in your human spirit, housed in your physical body.

God's Kingdom Operates Through the Human Spirit

The word *kingdom* means "domain." The Kingdom of God is the place in which God has dominion. It does not come with observation. The Kingdom of God came to earth when men were born again, when they received the new birth of the human spirit.

You learn to tap the power of the Kingdom by studying the Word of God. Remember, Jesus said, *Seek ye first the kingdom of God, and his righteousness; and all these things shall be added unto you.*

You have to seek first the Kingdom. Find where the Kingdom is and how the Kingdom operates.

The human spirit is where the Kingdom is set up, and it is capable of providing everything you need in this life, whether it be spiritual, physical, or financial. It is designed to either produce it, lead you to it, or cause it to come. You need to know how to allow your spirit to operate effectively in the Kingdom.

Your own spirit knows more than your intellect. Paul said, *For what man knoweth the things of a man, save the spirit of man which is in him* (1 Cor. 2:11). It is your human spirit—the real you, the man on the inside—who is in contact with God and knows all about you: your needs, failures, shortcomings, strong points. A man's intellect does not know all; but if you learn to tap into your spirit, which can tap the wisdom of God, then as Jesus said, all things will be added unto you. You will prosper.

When you were born again, it didn't take long for you to realize that your physical body didn't get born again. If your body had certain habits before you got saved, it wanted to continue those habits even after you were saved. It was your spirit man that was born again. You had to mortify the deeds of your body. (Rom. 8:13.)

It is vital that you realize the Kingdom, or the domain, of God is inside you! Your human spirit is born of the Spirit of God. You have the life of God in you. You have the Greater One inside you, so He is capable of exercising dominion in your spirit at your will.

He is *able to do exceeding abundantly above all that we ask or think, according to the power that worketh in us* (Eph. 3:20).

Things To Remember

The earth was designed to be a duplicate of heaven.
It is God's will for things to be
on earth as they are in heaven.

We don't have to pray *Thy kingdom come.*
The Kingdom has already come.

Jesus came to dwell in man through the Holy Spirit.
The Kingdom of God is within *you!*

6

Our Source of Supply

Whosoever cometh to me, and heareth my sayings, and doeth them, I will shew you to whom he is like... (Luke 6:47).

Jesus said that a man who *cometh to me, and heareth my sayings, and doeth them* digs deep and lays the foundation of his life on a rock, which is the Word of God. He bases his doings on what God's Word says and not on the world system.

To succeed physically, financially, and spiritually, we must obey God's Word. Jesus tells us what to do and how to do it. It is then up to us to follow instructions.

In Matthew 6:33 Jesus makes this statement: *Seek ye first the kingdom of God, and his righteousness; and all these things shall be added unto you.* In other words, first things first. Someone might say this is oversimplifying things, but I didn't say it—Jesus did!

God Wants To Supply Your Needs Here on Earth

Some people think when Jesus said, *...all these things shall be added unto you,* He meant when we get to heaven, not on earth. Don't let the Devil con you into believing that.

The story is told of a very wealthy man who died. When someone asked how much money he left, the lawyer replied,

"All of it." Heaven is a wealthy place. It is filled with abundance. You won't need money up there. You need it here on the earth. When you get to heaven, there will be nothing to buy, no demons to cast out, no sick to heal.

Many people believe when Jesus said, *Seek the kingdom,* He meant to look to the heavens. I thought that way for years. Then one day it occurred to me, "What am I going to do with it up there? There won't be anything to buy. There won't be any needs there. Gasoline won't be $1.30 a gallon and coffee won't be $5 a pound!"

I won't need money when I get to heaven. Paul said, *We brought nothing into this world, and it is certain we can carry nothing out* (1 Tim. 6:7).

It is in the earth today that we need the power of God and His anointing to gain riches. We need them *now* to preach the Gospel—not when we get to heaven! If you seek the Source, then all these things will be added to you. But it requires dedication.

God Will Grant Your Desires

Some people hesitate to totally commit themselves to God, to seek God's Kingdom first. They say, "If I sell out to God, He might send me to Africa, and I don't want to go."

That's not the way it works. James said if a man is a doer of the Word and not a hearer only, he will be blessed in his deeds; he will walk in *the perfect law of liberty.* (James 1:23,25.)

If you are totally sold out to God, determined to do His will and purpose without reservation to obey, then you will know God's will.

If you are totally committed to God, He will give you the desires of your heart. (Ps. 37:4,5.) He will put a desire in your heart for the very thing He wants you to do. Then you will be doing exactly what you want to do and be in His perfect will. Psalm 34:10 says, *They that seek the Lord shall not want any good thing.*

Let me give you an example. I had been a farmer for 28 years and I loved it. I had told people, "I'll never quit farming." It was the greatest desire of my heart. But when I sold out to God, He began to change my desires.

I didn't want to be a preacher because I had the wrong idea of preachers. But finally I told my wife, "I don't know where God is leading, but I'm going." It was several years before God required me to give up farming; but gradually, little by little, He changed my desires.

In 1979 I sold out of the farming business because the greatest desire of my heart was to teach and preach the Word of God. Today I am doing exactly what I want to do and I'm in the perfect will of God, because God has put His desire in my heart.

There are some people who go through life, even in the ministry, being obedient to all they know, but they never find what God wants them to do because they aren't willing to do it. It seems as though God will not reveal His complete will until you are willing to do it. If you get willing, God will change your desires and you will have joy doing it.

So many go through life miserable; they are obedient, but not willing. They are doing it because they know it is required of them. They never do the perfect will of God because they aren't willing to really sell out to God. Then you have people who are willing, but somehow they just never get around to doing it. Both of these are miserable throughout life.

You will never find out what God really has in store for you unless you are willing to go wherever He leads you. Once you become willing, He will change your desires.

Put God Before Things

In order for your desires to be the same as God's, you must be committed to seeking God, not those desires.

In Matthew 6:24, Jesus said, *No man can serve two masters: for either he will hate the one, and love the other; or else he will hold to the one, and despise the other. Ye cannot serve God and mammon.* This simply means that you cannot serve both God and riches. You must choose to serve God and make riches serve you.

If you go lusting after riches, you will fail in life. Second Peter 1:4 says, *Whereby are given unto us exceeding great and precious promises: that by these ye might be partakers of the divine nature, having escaped the corruption that is in the world through lust.*

If you say, "I'm going to be rich and be Mr. Big," you will fail.

There is no room for that kind of prosperity in God's plans. You might get it that way through the world's system, but it's not going to work with God. If your heart condemns you, your faith will not work. Wrong motives will shut down your faith.

They that will be rich fall into temptation and a snare, and into many foolish and hurtful lusts, which drown men in destruction and perdition. For the love of money is the root of all evil (1 Tim. 6:9,10).

It's the love of money that is the root of all evil, but there are people committing that sin—falling into temptation and snare—who don't have any money! They would kill you for $50! It's not money that's the sin; it's the love of it.

Jesus said, *A man's life consisteth not in the abundance of the things which he possesseth* (Luke 12:15). Paul urges us not to spend time seeking after things.

He says, *Godliness with contentment is great gain* (1 Tim. 6:6).

You must not make riches your god, but you can serve God and have riches. God wants His people to be wise in *every* area of their lives. You can serve God and have riches if you will use riches the way God intended. It is all right to have things, as long as things don't have you!

The key to being successful is simple. Act on the faith you have and do what Jesus said: Seek first the Kingdom of God and His righteousness. You must learn to seek the Source of supply. The Kingdom of God is the Source.

Things To Remember

*Seek ye first the kingdom of God, and his righteousness;
and all these things shall be added unto you.*

These *things* will be added to you on earth.

You won't need money in heaven.

If you seek God's Kingdom first,
you will know His will and
He will give you the desires of your heart.

Seek the Source, not the things!

Choose to serve God and make riches serve you!

7

Sell and Give

Sell that ye have, and give alms; provide yourselves bags which wax not old, a treasure in the heavens that faileth not, where no thief approacheth, neither moth corrupteth. For where your treasure is, there will your heart be also.

Luke 12:33,34

Jesus tells you in verse 33 how to operate in His Kingdom. If you are going to operate in the Kingdom of God, you must operate in Kingdom principles. Most Christians are failing because they are trying to operate the world system in the Kingdom of God. You have to operate Kingdom principles in the Kingdom. World system ways will not work in your spirit. You must use Kingdom principles, which are foreign to the world's way of thinking.

Sell that ye have. Jesus is ministering to all kinds of people. There are some poverty-stricken people in that crowd, and He says, *Sell that ye have.* In other words, "If you don't have anything to give, sell something and give."

Provide yourselves bags. Jesus didn't say to "provide for yourself with bags." He said to "provide yourselves bags." When the Bible speaks of "yourself" and the Apostle Paul speaks of "himself," they are referring to the inner man. The real you is the man on the inside—the spirit man, the human spirit.

Deposit God's Word in your spirit. Then speak forth God's Word from your heart. A good man out of the good treasure of his heart will bring forth good things.

As an example, let's take the scripture verse Luke 6:38. Begin to say, "Thank God, because I have given, it is given unto me good measure, pressed down, shaken together, and running over." Speak it. Make it a daily confession. Bring it forth with the words of your mouth.

God is honest; He will perform His Word. He said, "My Word will not return unto Me void." (Isa. 55:11.) But God wants you to return His Word to Him. So take God's Word— His promise concerning a specific thing. If your need is in the area of finances, put that Word in your heart by speaking it there. Get the good treasure of God's Word in your mouth, then speak it. That will bring it out and cause a manifestation.

Giving is one of the fundamental principles of the law of prosperity. It's not the amount given that is the greatest importance to God, but the percentage.

If you have five pennies and give one of them, you have given twenty percent of all that you own. To God that is just as important as a man who has five million dollars and gives a million. As far as God is concerned, that man hasn't given more than you have.

Rewards are based on percentages given. The return is based on the amount you give. This principle works for you the same as it does for the millionaire. The only difference is that he is operating with larger numbers. If you will continue using the principle, your nickel can turn into a million dollars!

Don't Eat Your Seed

Luke 6:38 says, *Give, and it shall be given unto you....* But some people eat their seed: They use all that they receive on themselves until they have nothing to give.

A good example of what happens when you eat your seed can be seen in the life of a man I met in Montana. He picked me up at the airport and drove me to a meeting. Though he did very little talking, I could tell everything was going wrong for him.

After the last meeting of the seminar, he came to me and said, "Brother Capps, my wife and I are in bad financial trouble. She doesn't have a job, and my job doesn't pay enough to meet the bills. I don't know what we're going to do!"

I said, "Let's pray."

Not knowing how to pray, I prayed in the Spirit. As I prayed, the Spirit of God said to me, "He has eaten his seed. He has taken money he should have given to the Gospel and used it for other things."

As I prayed for that man, the Lord said, "Give him $100. Then tell him not to spend it on himself, but to give it away."

He told me later that the Lord had already spoken to him about giving to two ministries. But he said, "I didn't have any money to give." He took the money I gave him and divided it between the two ministries.

About three months later when I went back to that town for another seminar, the man said, "I want to tell you what happened: I got a raise and my wife got a job! Our financial problems are over!"

Seeds Are for Planting

Any farmer knows if he eats his seed, he will be in trouble!

All God has to work with is what is sown or given. He can't produce a crop if we haven't given Him the seed to multiply. Make a habit of giving, whether your income is large or small.

Unless you give when your income is small, you will never give big. If you haven't developed the habit of giving tithes and offerings when you are making $90 a week, you will never do it when you are making $1,000 a week. We must be obedient to the basic principle which remains the same regardless of our income.

Jesus said if you don't have anything to give, sell what you have to get some seed.

You Reap on Earth

Sell that you have, and give alms; provide yourselves bags which wax not old, a treasure in the heavens that faileth not (Luke 12:33). Traditionally, we have misinterpreted this verse to mean that we are laying up treasures in heaven which are unavailable to us on earth. We won't need money in heaven; we need it here on earth.

Your Bag Is Your Spirit (Heart)

When Jesus said, *Provide yourselves bags which wax not old,* He didn't mean to get a purse that you would use in heaven!

What part of you doesn't get old? Paul said, *Though our outward man perish, yet the inward man is renewed day by day* (2 Cor. 4:16). According to Paul, the part of you that doesn't wax old is your human spirit. Your inward man is renewed day by day; it never ages.

The Greek word for *treasure* in Luke 12:33 means *deposit.* Jesus is saying that, by giving, you are providing yourself (the human spirit) as a bag, a purse, or a container, in which you store or deposit God's Word (the Treasure). Moths can't corrupt this bag; neither can thieves steal it because this container is the heart.

Jesus said, *For where your treasure is, there will your heart be also.* The treasure isn't being stored for you to get later in heaven. It's in your heart—the production center of God's Kingdom. This is God's Kingdom at work on the earth.

Your Need Has Been Supplied

Inflation is a thief, but it can't steal what you put in your heart. Put God's Word in your heart, and thieving circumstances will not be able to rob you. Confess daily:

"I have given, and it shall be given unto me. I sow bountifully; therefore, I'm reaping bountifully. My God meets all of my need according to His riches in glory by Christ Jesus."

Paul wrote the Philippian church and said, *My God shall supply all your need according to his riches in glory by Christ Jesus* (Phil. 4:19). He used the word *need,* not *needs.*

Prior to this, he had said, *...no church communicated with me as concerning giving and receiving, but ye only...ye sent once and again unto my necessity* (vv. 15,16). The Philippians had been obedient to the laws of prosperity and had hidden the good Word of God in their hearts. Because they gave to help Paul, God's servant, then God was promising to supply all their need. He was saying that their needs wouldn't pile up, but that they would have one need at a time and that He would meet each need as it came due.

The promise came because they had stored the Word of God in their hearts and acted on it by giving.

According to Luke 12:33, when we sell what we have and give alms, we are provided *a treasure in the heavens that faileth not.*

In the Bible, three different phrases are translated *heaven* or *heavens.* In this verse from Luke's Gospel, *heaven* refers to the lower level of heaven, which is just a little higher than the earth. The Greek word for *heavens* in Luke 12:33 doesn't mean the higher heaven where God is; it means the first level of heaven which is just above the world system.

The World's System Is Designed To Fail

God's system of success we are discussing is not positive thinking or a scheme dreamed up to work in the world system. It works in the spiritual realm. It works out of the human spirit, not out of man's intellect. If you only confess out of your head (your mind), the system won't work because it's a spiritual operation.

Provide yourselves bags which wax not old.... Let your spirit produce what you need. Let it be the ground in which you deposit the seed of God's Word. Out of that seed good things will grow and you will reap the harvest on earth.

...a treasure in the heavens that faileth not.... After all the world's schemes fail—when everybody is hiding in the mountains, storing up for the famine—God's system of sowing and reaping will prevail. The present world system is failing because it was designed to fail. God's system won't fail; it will prevail.

When everyone else has an empty gas tank, your tank will be running over because of the good seed you have sown in your heart.

Jesus says that it is unfailing on the higher plane where no thief approaches and no moth corrupts. (Luke 12:33.) We begin to think, *That must be in heaven because no thief can get up there and there will be no moths or insects there to corrupt it.* But wait a minute! He says, *Provide yourselves bags that wax not old.* How many ladies do you know whose purses are no older now than when they bought them? Jesus is saying, "Provide *yourself* as a container, a depository, that will never wax old."

You may say, "That must be in heaven." No. In 2 Corinthians 4:16 the Apostle Paul says, *...but though our outward man perish, yet the inward man is renewed day by day.* Jesus was saying that you provide yourself. Your human spirit, which the Bible calls "the heart," becomes the container that you put the treasure in.

Now how do you put it in there? In Romans 10:18 Paul tells you: *The word is nigh thee, even in thy mouth, and in thy heart.* First *in thy mouth,* then *in thy heart.* It gets in your mouth before it gets in your heart. The psalmist David said, *...my tongue is the pen of a ready writer* (Ps. 45:1). Proverbs 3:3 refers to writing *upon the table of thine heart. How* do you do it? With the tongue. The tongue is the instrument that writes on the heart.

When we operate in the realm of the spirit with God the Father, we will find the wisdom of God to bring our prosperity on earth.

Consider the account of the prophet Elisha in 2 Kings 6:1-6. When he and the sons of the prophets went out to cut down some poles at the edge of the Jordan, one of the ax heads flew off and sank in the river.

The prophet Elisha cut a stick and threw it in the water where the ax head had sunk.

The people standing around must have wondered, "What in the world is he doing?"

Elisha used the stick to cause something to happen: The ax head floated to the top! Under the world's system ax heads don't float, but Elisha was operating in the spirit realm. An ax head floating on water is a spiritual operation that cannot be explained in natural terms.

When you operate in the spirit realm, the people around you who operate in the natural realm will react to you just like the people reacted to Elisha. They'll say, "What in the world is he doing by confessing abundance and no lack? The news tells us that inflation is eating up our bank accounts!"

People have told me, "God's not concerned about material things."

Isn't an ax head a material thing? There is certainly nothing spiritual about it! God produces miracles of like substance. When Elisha wanted the ax to float, he threw something in the water that would float and received a miracle of like substance.

God's System Produces Abundance

We must realize that God designed a system in the earth, in you, that will produce everything you need in this life— not just enough to barely get along, but more than enough so that you can live the abundant life!

You must work the system diligently; otherwise, it won't produce for you, just as the world system won't produce for the man who is too lazy to work at it.

Some people can start with nothing and make a million dollars. Why? Because they know how to operate the world system. Others, not diligent in operating the world system of business, could start with a million dollars but lose it to someone who applies himself in the ways of the world.

Operate in the Spiritual Realm

God's principles, which operate on a spiritual plane, put a positive charge around you and ward off all that the Devil can send against you. This faith force, which works on a higher plane, causes the blessings of God to come to you when everyone else is in lack.

Knowing how to live on that higher plane is worth digging for in the Word of God. Jesus said that you are providing a treasure on a higher plane that *will fail not.* That treasure won't fail *when it's on that higher plane.*

If you drag the supernatural principles down to the level of the world, they will fail. If you say, "This system doesn't look as though it's going to work!" you're dragging the spiritual principles down to the level of what you see, feel, and hear. They won't work!

Apply the giving principle to small matters first until you learn how to give successfully. It will work just as well to get you a parking place downtown as it will to bring in $50,000 to pay a note. God's way is a miracle of like substance. No matter what you give up—whether it's money or your parking place—it works by the same principle.

Things To Remember

Giving is one of the fundamental principles
of the laws of prosperity.

Rewards are based on the percentages given.

Don't eat your seed!

Make a habit of giving.
If you don't have anything to give, sell something.

By giving, you are providing yourself (your spirit) as a bag.
You deposit God's Word in your spirit by speaking it.

The Word is in your mouth before it gets in your heart.

Operating in God's system will produce abundance in
your life. The blessings will come when others lack!

8

Speaking Kingdom Language

To put God's principles into motion and get them to work for you, you must spend time meditating God's Word.

In Joshua 1:8 God said to Joshua:

This book of the law shall not depart out of thy mouth; but thou shalt meditate therein day and night, that thou mayest observe to do according to all that is written therein: for then thou shalt make thy way prosperous, and then thou shalt have good success.

Picture yourself in Joshua's shoes. After Moses died, God put on Joshua the responsibility of leading three million people. These are the same people that murmured against Moses and said, *Would God that we had died...in the wilderness!* (Num. 14:2).

God instructed Joshua how to *have good success,* how he could *deal wisely* in all the affairs of life. God told him to be motivated by His Word: *This book of the law* (the Word of God) *shall not depart out of thy mouth.* In other words, Joshua was to keep saying what God said.

In Deuteronomy 28:1-2 God said, *If thou shalt hearken diligently unto the voice of the Lord thy God...all these blessings shall come upon thee, and overtake thee.*

Again, this means that the way to have success is to keep speaking God's Word.

Meditate the Word

God told Joshua to *meditate therein* (in the Word) *day and night.* Meditating the Word is vital for prospering the soul.

Meditate means "to dwell on, think on; to mutter or speak to one's self." A secret of success lies in this definition!

God was telling Joshua to get it inside him by quoting what God said with his own voice. By "meditating day and night," God didn't mean that Joshua would never sleep. He meant that Joshua was to meditate the Word during his waking hours and when he lay down to sleep.

If you go to sleep meditating on God's Word, you can have the things of God before you continually in your spirit at night.

Meditate therein day and night, that mayest observe to do according to all that is written therein: for then thou shalt make thy way prosperous.

Prosperity God's Way

Who was going to make Joshua's way prosperous? *Joshua!* He was the one who would determine his success.

Some people look for someone else to blame. God said that Joshua would make his way prosperous if he did what God said to do. That doesn't mean that God had nothing to do with Joshua's prosperity. It was God's Word that was causing the prosperity, but Joshua had to speak it.

Give God's Word first place in your life. Meditate it. Dwell on it. Speak it to yourself. Quote it. It will build a shield of faith around you. (Eph. 6:16.)

God's Word Builds a Faith Shield

Finally, my brethren, be strong in the Lord, and in the power of his might...take unto you the whole armour of God, that ye may be able to withstand in the evil day, and having done all, to stand.

Stand therefore, having your loins girt about with truth, and having on the breastplate of righteousness;

And your feet shod with the preparation of the gospel of peace;

Above all, taking the shield of faith, wherewith ye shall be able to quench all the fiery darts of the wicked.

Ephesians 6:10,13-16

Once, while praying in the Spirit, I saw that the shield of faith was different from the shield the Roman soldiers used. Their shield was only effective where it was held; the enemy could come behind it. The shield of faith is to quench every fiery dart of the wicked one!

The faith shield is created by the words of your mouth. It is as a canopy which spreads out around you from your head to your feet! This atmosphere radiates from you and will stop whatever the Devil brings against you.

You can compare this shield to a magnet with a positive charge. If you lay some tacks out on a desk and run a magnet over them, they will stick to it. Faith attracts God's blessings to you in the same way a magnet draws metal. You will naturally attract any blessing within miles.

On the other hand, a negatively charged magnet, placed in the center of the tacks, will repel all of them. You can't move the magnet fast enough to get even one tack to touch it!

Someone may say, "I don't know why God lets some people have all the blessings. Good deals never come my way!" That person is radiating a negative charge. He could be in the center of a pool of blessings and be repelling them because of the negative charge he is releasing.

A negative charge of fear and doubt will cause the blessings of God to flee from you.

Some people read Ephesians 6:16 this way: "Taking the shield of *doubt,* wherewith ye shall be able to quench all the *blessings of God!*"

That verse says to take the shield of *faith* and quench the *fiery darts of the enemy.* This is not a theory; it is a law of God's Word!

Charge Your Magnet Positively

To create the positive charge of faith that will draw God's blessings, you must meditate in God's Word.

A positively charged atmosphere takes time to develop. It takes months to get it into your spirit.

When I first read the promise of God to Abraham in the Covenant (Gen. 17), I thought, *So, God made a promise to Abraham. What good does that do me?* There was a lack of knowledge on my part. I didn't realize I was included; but when I found out that I could operate in it, I began to make faith statements to create a positive charge around me.

A man with a negative charge in him is positive about negative things and negative about positive things. He believes that *all negative things* are going to *come his way.* If he got a raise the first of the month, he would say, "Watch and see. We'll probably have a doctor's bill that will take all the extra money!"

That man just opened the door to the Devil! No matter what good comes his way, he always finds something evil to say about it.

It seems as though every bad thing that comes down the road stops at his house! That causes him to become more negative. That negative charge will repel blessings and draw negative things to him! He sets up a force field around him by what he speaks, either positive or negative.

You don't see words coming out your mouth; you grasp mental images as a result of hearing your words.

Words Are Spirit Life

Words are spiritual forces. Jesus said in John 6:63, *It is the spirit that quickeneth; the flesh profiteth nothing: the words that I speak unto you, they are spirit, and they are life.*

Words are spirit. Words created everything you can see, feel, taste, touch, or hear. Words—spiritual forces, spiritual power—created the whole universe!

You may say, "But that was God Who created the universe!"

But in Genesis 1:26 God said, *Let us make man in our image, after our likeness: and let them have dominion over the fish of the sea, and over the fowl of the air, and over...all the earth.* Verse 27 adds, *So God created man in his own image, in the image of God created he him; male and female created he them.*

God created us with the same capabilities of speaking spirit words! When Adam sinned, he became spiritually dead. He lost the ability to put spirit life into his words.

God says that the way to get words to work for you is to put His words in your mouth. This is the only way He could get spiritual life back into man's words.

For verily I say unto you, That whosoever shall say unto this mountain, Be thou removed, and be thou cast into the sea; and shall not doubt in his heart, but shall believe that those things which he saith shall come to pass; he shall have whatsoever he saith.

Mark 11:23

The Lord once told me, "I have told My people they can have what they say, and My people are saying what they have."

This statement is so simple, it's almost foolish; yet so profound, it's astounding.

As long as you say what you have, you will have what you say and no more. You will never have more than what you are saying, and you will never get out of the position you are in!

Jesus' words are spirit life. They are spiritual forces, sent out from you, which will draw the blessings of God to you. Remember what God told Israel: "If you will hearken diligently unto the voice of the Lord—declare wholly, completely, louder and louder, what I have said—all those blessings will come upon you and overtake you." This is the language of the Kingdom.

If blessings haven't overtaken you in the past, maybe it is because you were declaring, louder and louder, what the Devil said.

The only chance the Devil has to get you to radiate the wrong spiritual forces is through your words. If you radiate the forces of God in agreement with His Word, your circumstances will change and the Devil can't stop it.

You could walk into the middle of a bad situation, and the spiritual forces would cause the blessings of God to surround you. That will draw attention! People will stand around and say, "You are the luckiest guy who ever walked!" They call it luck, but it's the Word of God!

Speak Abundance Before the Need Arises

Meditate the Word to set God's system in motion before a major crisis ever comes along. God's principles will not only get you out of trouble, but they will *keep* you out of trouble. It's extremely difficult to pour a foundation when the flood is on. You must lay the foundation days and weeks before you start building.

Start now to proclaim: "My God supplies all my need according to His riches in glory. I have abundance." Start saying it now *before* the need arises. Before sickness comes, say, "Thank God, I'm healed by Jesus' stripes! I'm delivered from the powers of darkness."

The time to begin making your confession is not after everything has gone wrong. It takes longer to work these principles if a problem is already upon you, because you have to combat thoughts and imaginations. It also takes time to build the Word into your spirit.

It is much easier to believe you are walking in divine health when your body is not hurting. If you are sick, it's all right for you to have hands laid on you or go to a doctor; but God's best for us is to walk in divine health.

God's will in heaven is that there be no sickness or disease. Your faith won't eliminate sickness and disease from the earth; but by continually speaking the Word of God, it is possible to eliminate it from your house.

Jesus taught His disciples to pray, *Thy will be done in earth, as it is in heaven.* Avoid going through a "wilderness experience" by laying the foundation of the Word *before* problems arise. Use your faith on the front end of things!

Speak out your confession of faith when you have no sickness or financial problems. "Thank God, my God meets all my need!" You are building strength into your inner man.

If you see a problem coming, speak to it and command it to be removed. Resist it like you would resist the Devil.

Confess God's Word concerning prosperity regularly. If you drift along thinking things are going so well that you don't need to keep up your confession, you may wake up one morning and find yourself suddenly facing a financial crisis. If you start speaking to the problem then (as you should have been doing all along), you may have to live with the situation until the laws have time to work.

How long should you keep confessing the Word of God? Until Jesus comes! *Confess it daily.* Make it a way of life to speak forth abundance before a need arises. By continually speaking what God says, you are continually keeping His Word working in your finances and in your physical body.

Prosper Your Soul

Meditating the Word—speaking abundance before a need arises—causes your soulish man to prosper which, in turn, brings it in line with your spirit man (the inner man). You will so establish the prosperity of your soul that you will resist the first symptom that hits your body as you would resist the Devil! You will automatically say, "No, in the name of Jesus, you stop! I don't allow that in my body."

The same principle holds true for lack. At the first symptom of lack, speak out boldly, "In the name of Jesus, I command you to depart. My God supplies my need!"

You may find yourself seeing the truth in these areas, but not acting on them. If you meditate on them and *the Word on which they are based,* you will be motivated by them.

Words Will Heal or Kill

Even those in medical science have found Proverbs 18:21 to be true: *Death and life are in the power of the tongue.*

Recently, I heard of a doctor who told of a situation that occurred in his practice. When he told one of his patients that she must have an operation, she said, "If you operate on me, I'll die!" Because of that, he would not perform the needed surgery. He dismissed her from the hospital.

Later, a young colleague approached the doctor and said, "I heard you dismissed that patient who you said must have an operation. Why?"

The doctor said, "I wouldn't touch her because she was speaking things that would bring death!" That doctor was aware of the power of words.

There is a neurosurgeon in Wisconsin who treats people by word therapy. He has patients do what he calls *mental exercises* for fifteen minutes a day.

For example, someone with high blood pressure says for fifteen minutes a day: "My blood pressure is one hundred and twenty over eighty." The doctor said, "Whether or not that patient understands what he is saying makes no difference; his body knows and will obey him!"

A person with sugar diabetes says for fifteen minutes every day: "My pancreas secretes sufficient insulin for this body."

The neurosurgeon stated that the patient does not have to know what his pancreas is or does; his body knows and will obey his voice. He said, "I don't know *why* it works, but it does!"

The why is *Mark 11:23!* It has taken medical science two thousand years to find out that Jesus knew what He was talking about!

The doctor gave as an illustration a hopeless case—a lady who had terminal cancer. The doctors had done all they could for her. She had been in terrible pain; but after three weeks of word therapy, all the pain left her body! Three months later X rays showed no sign of cancer. She was totally healed!

This is not mind over matter; it is God's Word over all matter. God told Adam to have dominion, and that dominion was through his words. Confess daily that every disease germ and virus that touches your body will die instantly! Subdue it and have dominion over it.

Some people may say, "You must think you're God," just because you will not bow to all the circumstances of life!

Jesus said, *If ye had faith as a grain of mustard seed, ye might say unto this sycamine tree, Be thou plucked up by the root, and be thou planted in the sea; and it should obey you.*

Words created your body. Words created everything. Jesus said the sycamine tree would obey you! The sycamine tree isn't smarter than your body; it is an inanimate object. It will obey. Circumstances will obey you. Words will affect your body. They will cause you to be healed or remain sick.

Medical science discovered years ago that about 70 percent of all sickness comes from what people say or do. Many sicknesses are spiritual. For example, getting into strife or harboring unforgiveness are spiritual problems, but they can cause physical problems.

Medical Cures Through Words

In the days to come, the medical profession is going to find cures for dreaded diseases like bone disease, and the cures are going to come predominately from the book of Proverbs.

Many of these diseases and problems will be cured only when people straighten out their language and put perverse lips far from them.

The heart of the wise teacheth his mouth, and addeth learning to his lips. Pleasant words are as an honeycomb, sweet to the soul, and health to the bones (Prov. 16:23,24).

A merry heart doeth good like a medicine: but a broken spirit drieth the bones (Prov. 17:22).

The words you speak are powerful! They can be healing forces. They can minister to you life or death.

Things To Remember

Success comes as you meditate and speak God's Word.

You are the one who determines your success.

Giving God's Word first place in your life
builds a shield of faith around you.

Speaking faith-filled words attracts God's blessings
to you the same way a magnet draws metal.

Speak abundance *before* the need arises.

If you see a problem coming, speak to it
and command it to be removed.

Resist lack like you would resist the Devil.

Keep God's Word in your mouth until Jesus comes!
Make this a way of life!

9

Dominion Through the Kingdom

Adam had the knowledge of *all* good; he tapped into revelation knowledge of God's Spirit. All that he gained by eating of that tree in the Garden was knowledge of calamity and how to produce it by the words of his mouth.

Satan failed to tell Adam: "The day you eat of the tree of blessing and calamity, you'll not only gain knowledge of how to produce calamity by the words of your mouth, but you'll lose control of your tongue! You'll be ruled by an evil force!"

The Tongue Governs the Heart

My brethren, be not many masters, knowing that we shall receive the greater condemnation. For in many things we offend all. If any man offend not in word, the same is a perfect man, and able also to bridle the whole body.

James 3:1,2

The perfect (or mature) man is one who doesn't offend in *word*. The Greek says, "If he does not stumble in his words, he is a perfect man, and able to bridle the whole body." *The Amplified Bible* says he will be able to "curb his entire nature."

Behold, we put bits in the horses' mouths, that they may obey us; and we turn about their whole body.

Behold also the ships, which though they be so great, and are driven of fierce winds, yet are they turned about with a very small helm, whithersoever the governor listeth.

James 3:3,4

The heart is the governor, but the tongue is what programs the governor. Words are extremely powerful because your tongue governs your heart!

James is saying that a bit in a horse's mouth will turn his whole body. A bit puts pressure on the tongue. The words you are saying will turn you about. Financially, you could be on the brink of disaster. If you will straighten out your words— put pressure on your tongue—you will change your course! The heart produces what you plant in it.

Your tongue is the rudder of your ship. If you don't like where you are, turn the rudder.

Man Can Tame the Tongue

When Adam sinned, he broke that communication link of the word between God and man. From my study of both Old and New Testaments, I am convinced that Adam's fall was directly connected to his tongue. When Adam ate the forbidden fruit, it poisoned his tongue.

Even so the tongue is a little member, and boasteth great things. Behold, how great a matter a little fire kindleth!

And the tongue is a fire, a world of iniquity, so is the tongue among our members, that it defileth the whole body, and setteth on fire the course of nature; and it is set on fire of hell.

James 3:5,6

James 3:8 states that the tongue is an *unruly evil, and full of deadly poison*. God didn't set it on fire; the Devil did! Man was capable of tapping the tree of life with his tongue in the Garden, and he is still capable of doing that today. The Word says, *A wholesome tongue is a tree of life: but perverseness therein is a breach in the spirit* (Prov. 15:4).

The Amplified Bible states James 3:6 this way: "The tongue sets on fire the wheel of birth—the cycle of man's nature...." In other words, if you inherited good health from your parents, more than likely you will be healthy—unless you don't control your tongue! Your tongue can change that nature you inherited!

There is healing power in your body; God created man that way. If you cut your finger, you don't have to stay up all night praying and hoping to God that it will heal. You don't know how it does it, but it will heal itself.

All those vessels will knit together and healing will come, unless you start saying, "I believe it's getting infected! It's looking worse every day! Just watch and see! I'll probably end up going to the doctor."

By speaking that way, you can stop the healing power that is in your body. Speaking those words into your heart will shut off the healing power. The inner man sends out an impulse that says, "Shut off the healing power; he's getting an infection!"

Jesus said whatever a man says will come to pass if he doesn't doubt in his heart. Your body was created to obey your words, and it knows how.

If the tongue is an unruly evil, full of deadly poison, set on fire of hell, who can be wholesome in their tongue? No man can tame it! But to prosper physically or financially, the tongue must be controlled.

God's Spirit and the Word Tame the Tongue

Man by his natural ability has tamed the birds, the beasts, and the fish of the sea; but no man with natural ability can tame the tongue. It takes supernatural ability, and the Word of God is supernatural ability.

It takes the Spirit of God to tame the tongue. It takes God within you for you to say, "My God has met my need according to His riches in glory," when it looks like your need being supplied is the farthest thing from the truth!

It takes the Spirit of God within you to rise up for you to say, "In the name of Jesus, that child playing in the street will not get run over! In the name of Jesus, that man's tire will not blow out before he gets to a filling station!"

You've heard people say, "Look at that guy! He's going to blow that tire off the rim before he goes another mile!"

Do you realize why God has not turned up the power on your words? If He had, you would have blown that man's tire off the rim! Then if you had said, "That car is going to fall apart before it gets off the freeway," you would have caused a serious accident. This is the reason we must develop our faith in a creative manner.

We must learn to use our words creatively. It takes God within us to control our tongues.

Idle Words

Either make the tree good, and his fruit good or else make the tree corrupt, and his fruit corrupt: for the tree is known by his fruit.

O generation of vipers, how can ye, being evil, speak good things? for out of the abundance of the heart the mouth speaketh.

Matthew 12:33,34

Jesus was addressing people who were speaking against Him. When you study these verses in context, you will discover that He is telling them they will not be let off on earth or in the world to come.

Some have taken this passage out of context and have misinterpreted it, thinking that Jesus said these men were eternally damned to hell. He wasn't saying that.

Idle Words Blaspheme the Holy Ghost

Jesus had just finished telling the people that He would forgive all manner of blasphemy except that which was against the Holy Ghost. *Whosoever speaketh against the Holy Ghost* (Matt. 12:32) is blaspheming against the Holy Ghost. In this scripture Jesus is saying: If you speak against the Word of God, which is authored by the Holy Ghost, you are blaspheming (speaking) against the Holy Ghost and you won't be let off for that; you will have the results of what you said.

There is a sin unto death. (See 1 John 5:16; Heb. 6:4-6; Heb. 10:26-29.) But the blasphemy against the Holy Ghost mentioned in Matthew 12:32 won't necessarily send you to hell. Every Christian has done it at some time. But if you contradict the Word of God continually, you are walking in dangerous territory.

Jesus said in Matthew 5:22, *Whosoever shall say, Thou fool, shall be in danger of hell fire.* Traditionally, we have thought this verse referred to the unpardonable sin in which your soul is damned to hell. But later Jesus Himself said, *O fools, and slow of heart...* (Luke 24:25). So by most interpretations of that scripture, Jesus was headed for hell. No, what Jesus was saying in Matthew 5:22 was that you won't be let off for speaking against what the Holy Spirit has authored.

The blood of Jesus was shed for our forgiveness. ...*All manner of sin and blasphemy shall be forgiven unto men* (Matt. 12:31), including blasphemy against Jesus.

According to what Jesus said in Matthew 12:32, *Whosoever speaketh a word against the Son of man, it shall be forgiven him.* In verse 31 He states: *But the blasphemy against the Holy Ghost shall not be forgiven unto men.* Jesus said **blasphemy** against the Holy Ghost—not sin.

The Pharisees were speaking against Jesus. They said Jesus had a devil and that He cast out devils by the prince of devils. (Matt. 9:34.) The Pharisees could not have been guilty of sinning against the Holy Ghost; they didn't even know the Holy Ghost existed. To be guilty of that, they first would have had to have knowledge of the Holy Ghost.

But they were speaking contrary to God's Word. Jesus said, "You won't be let off for that." The Pharisees received none of the miracles that others received because they didn't believe in them. Because of what they said, they received no healing or deliverance.

Jesus is simply saying that speaking contrary to what the Holy Ghost has authored will not be forgiven you on this earth. Jesus confirms this in Mark 11:23: *Whosoever shall say...and shall not doubt in his heart, but shall believe those things which he saith shall come to pass; he shall have whatsoever he saith.*

In other words, you will reap the results of what you say.

Satan has blinded the minds of people as to the Kingdom's operation, but ignorance won't excuse you in earth or in heaven. You will suffer the consequences for what you said by losing things you could have had on earth and, as a result, will lose rewards in heaven. Eventually, you will have what you say, whether right or wrong.

Whether you realize it or not, you are operating a divine principle of the Kingdom. Words are seeds in the spirit world; and they will bring to pass the things spoken.

A good man out of the good treasure of the heart bringeth forth good and an evil man out of the evil bringeth forth evil things (Matt. 12:35). When Jesus used the term *evil man,* He wasn't necessarily talking about a wicked man. He was referring to a man who allows his whole body to be full of darkness by getting an evil eye. You can do that by speaking negative things. (Matt. 6:23.)

An Evil Report

In the Book of Numbers, we find an example of what God called an evil report. The ten spies, who were sent into

Canaan to spy out the land, came back with this report: "We can't take the land. There are giants there." (Num. 13:27-33.) God called what they said *an evil report.* **In God's eyes, anything spoken contrary to God's Word, or Covenant, is an evil report.**

The ten spies described what they saw, felt, and heard. Their report was evil because it was based on the sense realm.

Many church members do not understand the principles of confession of faith. They say, "I'm being truthful when I say it like it is: I'm taking the flu; I can't pay my bills; I can't understand the Bible; I'll never have anything."

But any statement like that is an evil report because it is contrary to what God said. He said you are redeemed from the curse of the Law, and the blessing of Abraham is yours.

You Will Be Held Accountable

God considers any report that disagrees with Him to be evil.

Jesus says, I say unto you, That every idle word that men shall speak, they shall give account thereof in the day of judgment (Matt. 12:36).

Idle means "non-working." An idle word is any word you speak that doesn't work *for you.* Idle words usually contradict God's Word or give place to the Devil. If you make statements like, "I've prayed, but it's not working," or "We'll never get out of debt!" you won't be let off in this world or in the world to come because you are speaking words contrary to the Scriptures. The Word says in Psalm 1:3, *Whatever he doeth shall prosper.*

When we get to heaven, there will be those who have lost rewards, because they did not believe the Word of God to receive the things God provided for them in this life. They will say, "Lord, I didn't have money to give to that missionary because I could never hold a job. No matter what I did, I lost my job. I never had enough to give."

Jesus will say, "That was your problem while you were on earth. The very words you are saying will testify against you."

You will give account and lose reward for saying words which weren't God's words!

He will say, "You could have said things like this: *Whatever I do will prosper. No weapon formed against me will prosper. I'm delivered from the powers of darkness. I have overcome the world, the flesh, and the Devil, for the Greater One dwells in me. My God meets my need according to His riches in glory by Christ Jesus.*"

"But, Lord, it didn't look like it was true."

"Oh, so you walked by sight and not by faith."

Revelation 7:17 says that God is going to wipe away *all tears from their eyes.* When many see what they could have had, and what they get, they will cry! God will wipe away the tears and the knowledge of what you missed, but on Judgment Day you will give account of every idle word you ever spoke.

Learn to put a zipper on your mouth until you learn the language of the Kingdom. The vocabulary of silence will win many battles.

I have been in situations in which I couldn't say anything good, so I just gritted my teeth and didn't say anything. You will give an account of every non-working word. Learn to speak every word in a manner that will work for you.

By thy words thou shalt be justified, and thy words thou shalt be condemned (Matt. 12:37). You will be justified or condemned on the basis of the kind of words you decide to speak. Seed is sown by speaking words.

Remember, the law of faith also works in reverse. Every idle word you speak works *against* you, not for you.

The Law Will Work in Reverse

Some people say, "I believe I can have what I say if I speak good things. Surely God wouldn't let Mark 11:23 work in reverse!"

The very principle of it tells you it will work either way, just like the forward and reverse gears of your car. When you put the car in reverse, the car goes backward. If you had wanted to go forward, you will find out why you didn't when you see that the indicator is pointing to "reverse."

We wouldn't intentionally put a car in reverse when we want to go forward, yet many people operate the faith principle in a similar way. They pray the problem, talk the problem, and keep it before them day and night, even wake up in the middle of the night thinking about it. Then they wonder why they can never find a solution to the problem. They are trying to go forward with the principle in reverse!

Foolish Talk Confuses the Spirit

Keep thy heart with all diligence; for out of it are the issues of life.

Put away from thee a froward mouth, and perverse lips put far from thee.

Proverbs 4:23,24

Perverse lips means "willful and contrary speech." Perverse lips is speech contrary to what God's Word says, such as, "No matter what I do, nothing ever works out anymore!" This talk is contrary to what God's Word says; it's an evil report.

God says of the person who delights in God's Word: *Whatever he doeth will prosper, and he shall have whatsoever he saith.* (Ps. 1:3; Mark 11:23,24.) We have available to us the promises and ability of God. We are able to use these abilities to cause His Word to come to pass.

Be Careful When You Joke!

Be careful what you put into your heart. Even things you say jokingly will get into your spirit.

Many people are confusing their inner man by speaking out opposites of the truth. For example, someone may say, "Man, isn't it cold today!" when it's actually 102°.

Your faith will be less effective because of confusion in the spirit man. You must have continuity between what you are speaking and believing.

Resist making statements such as, "Isn't that a big dog!" when it is a little dog. These statements can confuse the heart and eventually cripple your faith. Saying it's hot outside when it's really cold, referring to a little dog as a big one, saying nothing ever works for you—all are examples of speaking with perverse lips.

Control Your Vocabulary

The little things people say and do get them into trouble. They are hindering their faith by sowing the wrong kind of seed.

God's Word is His will for you. Your word should be your will toward God. Never speak anything with your mouth that is not your will. You were designed to speak what you desire.

Most people don't have any faith in their words. You must develop yourself to control your vocabulary. If you talk all kinds of foolishness continually—saying perverse things— you will have no faith in your words!

When it comes time for you to speak a word of faith, nothing will happen. *Develop* yourself in it; say *only* what you believe shall come to pass.

Exercising diligence over your words puts the law of faith in motion.

> *If any man among you seem to be religious and bridleth not his tongue, but his deceiveth his own heart, this man's religion is vain.*

James 1:26

If you don't bridle your tongue, it will deceive your heart into believing that what you say is what you want. Once you are highly developed in believing what you say will come to pass, and you say something in jest, your spirit will search for a way to cause what you said to come to pass—even though you really didn't want it to come to pass.

If you are always saying, "We're going to go bankrupt for sure!" your spirit will search the wisdom of God to find a way to bring it to pass. Your heart (spirit) takes your words as final authority. Your words will deceive your heart to believe that bankruptcy is what you ordered. The seed has been planted.

Things To Remember

As you speak words—whether good or bad—
you are operating a divine principle of the Kingdom.

Words are seeds in the spirit world, and
they will bring to pass the things spoken.

Words are powerful because your tongue
governs your heart. To prosper in any area,
you must practice tongue control.

God's Word *is* supernatural ability!

To speak against the Word of God is
to speak against the Holy Ghost!

God considers any statement that disagrees
with His Word to be an evil report.

Idle words usually contradict God's Word.

You will give account for the idle words you speak.

Never speak anything that is not your will.

Exercise diligence over the words you speak.

Learn the vocabulary of silence!

10

Sowing Seed in the Kingdom

The Kingdom of God operates on the principle of sowing and reaping. The Kingdom of God within is the production center or source. In the parable of the sower from Mark's Gospel, chapter 4, Jesus tells us the heart is the soil which produces whatever you plant in it.

Hearken; Behold, there went out a sower to sow:

And it came to pass, as he sowed, some fell by the way side, and the fowls of the air came and devoured it up.

And some fell on stony ground, where it had not much earth; and immediately it sprang up because it had no depth of earth: but when the sun was up, it was scorched; and because it had no root, it withered away.

And some fell among thorns, and the thorns grew up, and choked it, and it yielded no fruit.

And other fell on good ground, and did yield fruit that sprang up and increased; and brought forth, some thirty, and some sixty, and some an hundred.

And he said unto them, He that hath ears to hear, let him hear.

*And when he was alone, they that were about him with the twelve asked of him the parable. And he said unto them, Unto you **it is given to know the mystery of the*** *kingdom of God:* *but unto them that are without, all these things are done in parables.*

Mark 4:3-11

After Jesus had shared this parable with His disciples, they asked Him why He spoke to them this way. He said, *Unto you it is given to know the mystery of the kingdom of God.*

Jesus spoke in parables in order to hide the revelation knowledge of God's truth from the people of the world who were not seeking after it and would not understand it.

He hid these truths in the Word so that we could find them. He is telling us to seek out the Kingdom and learn how it operates. When we do, it will cause all these other things that God hath given to be added to us.

Jesus' interpretation of this parable begins with verse 13: *And he said unto them, Know ye not this parable? and how then will ye know all parables?* In other words, "If you don't get this one, you're not going to understand any of them. You won't understand about the Kingdom because this parable lays the groundwork for all the others."

Words Are the Seed

In verse 14 Jesus says, *The sower soweth the word.*

There is a twofold application of this: Jesus is talking specifically about sowing the Word of God, but you can draw a parallel from that and say, "The sower sows words." The person Jesus was speaking of was not sowing natural seed at all; he was sowing words.

By the Way Side

And these are they by the way side, where the word is sown; but when they have heard, Satan cometh immediately, and taketh away the word that was sown in their hearts (v. 15).

Matthew's Gospel says it this way: *When any one heareth the word of the kingdom, and understandeth it not, then cometh the wicked one...* (Matt. 13:19).

If you hear the Word of God but don't understand it, then Satan is capable of coming in and stealing it from you. I am convinced also that if you don't act on the Word, Satan will steal it from you. We have to be *doers* of the Word, not just *hearers.* (James 1:22.)

Jesus said, *Satan cometh immediately, and taketh away the word that was sown in their hearts.* Immediately!

Where was the Word sown? In the hearts of the people.

Stony Ground

And these are they likewise which are sown on stony ground; who, when they heard the word, immediately receive it with gladness;

And have no root in themselves, and so endure but for a time: afterward, when affliction or persecution ariseth for the word's sake, immediately they are offended.

Mark 4:16,17

Here we have people who heard the Word, received it with joy, and walked in it for a while. But then affliction and persecution showed up and they quit.

The word *affliction* means "pressures of life." It could mean two dollars for a gallon of gasoline and five dollars for a pound of coffee. It could be sickness or disease. These are the pressures of life!

Jesus said, *...immediately they are offended.* They thought that God would change the prices for them.

A person hears, "When you give, God will give to you in return." He gets excited and suddenly decides to give away his car; then later he says, "I gave away my car. Why didn't God give me a new one?"

God is not necessarily obligated to give you a car. He may give you the money to buy one. If I am believing for a hundredfold return in my giving, I wouldn't give away my watch and expect to get a hundred watches in return. I wouldn't give away a car and believe for a hundred cars.

Believe God for the finances. You don't need a hundred cars. Keeping up a hundred cars could drain your bank account. It could be a curse instead of a blessing.

Sometimes, I think, we try to put God in a box. If you give something away, believe God for the finances to replace the item or to buy your own car. Don't lock God in a box. In doing so, you may miss it altogether.

Notice *why* afflictions and persecutions arise: *for the Word's* sake—not to make you strong, not to cause you to grow, but to get that Word out of you!

Among Thorns

And these are they which are sown among thorns; such as hear the word, and the cares of this world, and the deceitfulness of riches, and the lusts of other things entering in, choke the word, and it becometh unfruitful.

And these are they which are sown on good ground; such as hear the word, and receive it, and bring forth fruit, some thirtyfold, some sixty, and some an hundred.

Mark 4:18-20

When the Word was sown among thorns, the thorns sprang up and choked it. The thorns were already there, which tells us we need to do some *thorn pulling.*

If the thorns in your heart choke out the Word of God concerning prosperity, then you must get rid of the thorns. Get rid of those ideas which cause you to believe, "Maybe it's not God's will for me to prosper in a particular area." Meditate on God's Word concerning prosperity in the particular area you have a need. Get rid of the thorns, dig up the stones, then allow God's Word to take root in your heart.

Good Ground

Matthew 13:23 describes the man who received the seed into the good ground as one who *hears* the Word and *understands* it. Only one planting survived and brought forth fruit: the soil (heart) that received the seed. In other words, that soil was prepared; it had no thorns or stones in it.

The Soil

The sower is sowing words. Jesus said the soil that these words are sown into is the heart of man, or the human spirit. The heart is the *production center.* It is the soil that will produce what you plant.

The sower sows the seed of the Word of God. You are a sower. You sow God's Word into your heart by speaking His Word.

Faith Comes by Hearing

The first time you heard your voice on a tape recorder, you probably said, "That can't be me! It doesn't sound like me." But it *was* you, and it *did* sound like you! It sounded exactly the way you sound to everyone else. You were probably embarrassed by the way you sounded to yourself.

Why is that? The reason your voice does not sound the same to you on tape as when you are speaking is that on tape you are hearing yourself predominantly through the outer ear.

You have two sets of ears: the outer and the inner ear. The inner ear is a bone structure inside your head. When you talk, you get some sound through the outer ear; but most of the sound you hear comes through the inner ear. When you plug your ears and talk, the sound is louder because you are stopping up the outer ear.

That should tell us something. Paul wrote, *But the righteousness which is of faith speaketh...But what saith it? The word is nigh thee, even in thy mouth, and in the heart* (Rom 10:6,8). Notice the Word is in your mouth first, then in your heart.

I am convinced that God designed the physical body in such a way that the words you speak are picked up by the inner ear and fed directly into the human spirit. This is why the words *you* speak are so powerful.

Words spoken by someone else don't have that kind of effect on you. If I preached the Word of God to you and confessed what God said, you would get some faith from it if you accepted it into your spirit; but you would get it much faster if *you* started speaking it yourself. The words *you* say have more effect on your spirit than the words of another person.

Faith cometh by hearing, and hearing by the word of God (Rom. 10:17). One of the major keys to confession and faith is that what you hear yourself speak produces faith inside you.

Chapter 18 of Proverbs states: *The words of a man's mouth are as deep waters* (v. 4); *A fool's mouth is his destruction, and his lips are the snare of his soul* (v. 7); *A man's belly shall be satisfied with the fruit of his mouth; and with the increase of his lips shall he be filled* (v. 20).

As we have already seen, *belly* means "human spirit." A man's spirit shall be filled, or satisfied, with the fruit of his mouth. The way to fill your spirit is to speak. What you speak will get into your spirit.

When your words get into your spirit, they will get back into your mouth. Every time they go through this process they will get stronger. *Out of the abundance of the heart the mouth speaketh* (Matt. 12:34). The confession of God's Word is necessary to build faith.

Sow a Seed—Reap a Harvest

You sow seeds (words you speak) into the soil of your heart, into your spirit man. Every time you speak, you speak either God's words or the Devil's words. Each will produce after its kind.

Conceiving in the spirit is like planting seeds into soil. Just as a particular type of seed will bring forth that same kind of plant, so will a particular type of word produce after its kind.

This is the Law of Genesis. It has never changed, and it never will, for God made a promise to creation. In Genesis 8:21-22 the Lord said in His heart, *I will not again curse the ground any more for man's sake...While the earth remaineth, seedtime and harvest, and cold and heat, and summer and winter, and day and night shall not cease.*

In the covenant God made with Noah and the animals of the earth, He said that as long as the earth remained, the process of sowing and reaping would never cease.

Through the parable of the sower, God is telling us *how the Kingdom of God operates,* setting the stage for understanding how God's Kingdom works inside us. *It works by the sowing of words.* We plant words in the Kingdom of God which is in us.

Seeds Produce After Their Kind

You don't sow radish seeds in a garden and hope for cucumbers. When I was farming, I didn't plant cotton and expect to reap soybeans or rice. It just doesn't work that way.

While I was plowing the soil to plant cotton or soybeans, the ground never yelled at me and said, "I'm not going to raise soybeans this year. I've decided that you need cucumbers, so I'm going to raise cucumbers!"

It couldn't do that; it had to produce whatever I planted—whether it was cotton, soybeans, rag weeds, or oak trees! The soil had no choice but to do what the seed demanded.

About six months after a soybean seed is planted, it will produce a handful of soybeans that look just like the one planted. You can't plant soybeans and get apples, or plant cockelburs and get roses. The soil was not designed to decide what should be produced. God designed it to react to the demands of the seed that is planted and to bring forth an exact duplication of its kind.

The Heart Produces the Kind Planted

So is the kingdom of God, as if a man should cast seed into the ground; and should sleep, rise night and day, and the seed should spring and grow up, he knoweth not how (Mark 4:26,27).

Jesus is telling us that the heart, or spirit, of man was designed to operate in the same way that the ground produces crops. According to the Law of Genesis, everything produces after its kind.

We are seeking first the Kingdom by finding where the Kingdom resides, then how it works. We don't have to understand all the reasons why it works. We need to know how to plant the Word in the heart (soil), then once planted how to care for it to keep it from being choked. The soil will do the producing.

Your human spirit was designed to search the avenues of God's wisdom day and night—for years, if necessary—to lead you to the things or position you have been confessing.

Don't Sow Seed of Trouble

When you understand that your spirit continually produces what you speak, you realize why some bad things happen in your life. You can see that by saying things like, "Lord, we won't ever get these debts paid; we'll never have the money by the end of the year to make the house payment," you open the door to the Devil and allow that very thing to come to pass!

Some people say, "Trouble and sorrows follow me all the days of my life. I just get out of one, and another comes long. Every time I get ahead a little, something bad happens and it takes all our finances." These people don't realize that they have been saying this same thing twenty years and the Devil has had a heyday.

For several years Johnson grass was a problem on a portion of my farm. Johnson grass is a real problem to farmers and requires special attention. Suppose I had said to my workers, "Since we've had trouble with Johnson grass in this field, we're going to plant some more Johnson grass." It would be foolish for me to plant more grass or weeds just because I had been having trouble with weeds and grass. That doesn't make any sense at all, but many Christians are doing that very thing: praying and talking the problem. When you say, "Lord, I prayed and it's getting worse. What are we going to do?" you are sowing weed seed in the soil— and those seeds will produce. *Faith cometh by hearing.* They are hearing troubles and problems; therefore, they will have faith in the problems and troubles.

Some people continually sow seeds of doubt, fear, and unbelief. They talk sickness and disease, then wonder why they can't walk in prosperity and health. They may be crying out to God to change their situation; but as long as they continue to say the same things, God can't help them.

Everything produces after its kind. If they would speak according to the Word by making statements such as, "All the blessings in Deuteronomy 28 are coming upon me and overtaking me; goodness and mercy are following me all the days of my life," they would change the direction of their life. To turn your ship, you must turn the rudder. To change the harvest, you must change the seed you are sowing.

The Spirit Never Sleeps

The Apostle Paul said, *The Spirit itself beareth witness with our spirit, that we are the children of God* (Rom. 8:16).

You can't contact God with your body. God is a Spirit; therefore, we commune and fellowship with God through our spirits, even while we are asleep. Your spirit can commune with God 24 hours a day.

Whether you sow right seeds or wrong seeds, the principle of sowing and reaping will produce in your life. Learn the principles of how the Kingdom operates and apply them daily. They will not work for you just because you know about these principles. You must believe them and put them into action.

Things To Remember

God's Kingdom operates on the principle
of sowing and reaping.

Your heart is the soil.

The words you speak are the seeds.

You sow God's Word in your heart by
speaking it out your mouth.

Each time you speak, you are sowing words—
God's words or the Devil's words.

You will reap the harvest of your words,
whether good or evil.

You plant the Word; the soil will do the producing.
If you sow seeds of poverty and sickness,
the soil cannot produce prosperity and health.
To change the harvest,
you must change the seed you are sowing.

11

Supernatural Help by the Spoken Word

The first chapter of Hebrews describes two supernatural ministries that are available to us today: the ministry of Jesus and the ministry of angels. Jesus' ministry is much greater, but the angels play an important part in your life.

Let's take a look at the ministry of angels:

To which of the angels said he at any Sit on my right hand, until I make thine enemies thy footstool?

Are they not all ministering spirits, sent forth to minister for them who shall be heirs of salvation?

Hebrews 1:13,14

In this last verse, God was defining the role of the angels. They are ministering spirits. We are the heirs of salvation.

Continue now into chapter 2, verse 1: *Therefore we ought to give the more earnest heed to the things which we have heard, lest at any time we should let them slip.*

Don't let this truth slip from you. **The angels are ministering spirits, sent forth to minister for you.**

For if the word spoken by angels was stedfast, and every transgression and disobedience received just recompence of reward; how shall we escape, if we neglect so great salvation (vv. 2,3).

The word *salvation* means "deliverance, preservation, healing, and soundness." This verse refers to the deliverance that comes by the angels.

We shouldn't let it slip that the angels are ministering spirits sent to minister for us. How are we going to escape the things the Devil has set for us if we neglect the deliverance that comes by the angels? They are here to minister for us.

For instance, several years ago in Dallas, Texas, I was exiting off the freeway when I came upon a car that had stopped and blocked the way I was to turn, so I stopped. Another car, coming off the freeway, hit the back of my car. The gas tank burst and gasoline went everywhere, but there was no fire.

When my car was hit, I felt as though pillows were all around me. The angels were surrounding me as in Psalm 91:11: He has given His angels charge over me to keep me in all my ways. Verse 7 says, *A thousand shall fall at thy side, and ten thousand at thy right hand; but it shall not come nigh thee.*

Begin to believe and confess this daily. Apply this promise from the Word of God to your situation daily.

Notice what the angel said to John in 22:8-9: *I John saw these things, and heard them. And when I had heard and seen, I fell down to worship before the feet of the angel which shewed me these things. Then saith he unto me, See thou do it not: for **I am thy fellowservant....***

This angel said to John, *I am thy fellowservant.* The literal Greek says, "The fellow slave of yours I am." He said, "Don't worship me. I'm your servant."

...I am thy fellowservant, and of thy brethren the prophets, and of them which keep the sayings of this book.

The angels are here to serve us and bring us deliverance in time of danger.

How are you going to escape the snares of the enemy if you neglect so great a deliverance that came by angels?

When Daniel was in the lion's den, the angel shut the lion's mouth. (Dan. 6:22.) When Peter was in prison, the angel woke him up and led him out. (Acts 12:7.)

The Lord hath prepared his throne in the heavens; and his kingdom ruleth over all. Bless the Lord, ye his angels, that excel in strength, that do his commandments, hearkening unto the voice of his word (Ps. 103:19,20). The angels do God's commandments; and God's commandments are His statutes, His Word.

The angels are also involved in the Mark 11:23 faith principle: *He shall have whatsoever he saith.* If you are saying, believing and not doubting in your heart, then the angels are helping bring to pass your desires that agree with God's Word. The angels can't work on your behalf if your words don't line up with God's Word.

Your words either bind or loose your angels. When you say, "Nothing ever works for me; I never will get out of debt," you are binding your angels. They don't bring prosperity to you. They *do his commandments, hearkening unto the voice of his word,* but you didn't give voice to God's Word.

If you hold your Bible up to your ear, you can't hear a sound. The angels hearken to *the voice* of God's Word, and you are the one that must give it voice. You can give God's Word voice by saying:

"Blessed be God, I have given and it is given unto me—good measure, pressed down, shaken together, and running over. I have abundance; there is no lack. My God meets my need according to His riches in glory. The Lord is my Shepherd, and I do not want. I say, in the name of Jesus, that every disease germ and every virus that touches my body dies instantly. No weapon formed against me will prosper, and whatever I do will prosper."

Just remember: When you speak these words, the angels that have been waiting for you to give voice to God's Word will hearken to your voice. Yes, you have supernatural help available today by speaking God's Word.

Things To Remember

Angels are ministering spirits,
sent forth to minister for you.

They are here to serve you and
bring you deliverance in time of trouble.

The angels of God do His commandments.
They hearken unto the voice of His Word.

Your words will either bind or loose your angels.

Voice your desires in agreement with God's Word.

You must give God's Word voice.

12

Do the Sayings of Jesus

No one will be really successful in life unless he puts Jesus' sayings into action. Jesus said:

Whosoever cometh to me, and heareth my sayings and doeth them, I will shew you whom he is like:

He is like a man which built an house, and digged deep, and laid the foundation on a rock: and when the flood arose, the stream beat vehemently upon that house, and could not shake it: for it was founded upon a rock.

But he that heareth, and doeth not, is like a man that without a foundation built an house upon the earth: against which the stream did beat vehemently, and immediately it fell; and the ruin of that house was great.

Luke 6:47-49

Jesus is **not** talking about housing projects. He has revealed secrets that will make you successful in life. The Word says, *The secret things belong unto the Lord, our God: but those things which are revealed belong unto us* (Deut. 29:29).

Lay the Foundation with the Word

If we do the things Jesus says, we will have a firm foundation laid on a rock. When the stream beats upon our lives, the storm will not be able to shake us! However, Jesus said that if we don't do His sayings, we will be like the man who built his house on the sand. When the stream beat vehemently upon that house, *immediately it fell; and the ruin of that house was great.*

Some people have thought this scripture meant one of the men was saved and the other wasn't, but both men could have been saved. Both knew the truth, but only one did what Jesus said to do. The stream beating against his house *couldn't* shake it! He did not say it *didn't* shake it; He said it *couldn't.* It was impossible to destroy the one who was doing what Jesus said—he was resting on God's Word.

Doing the sayings of Jesus will transform your life! When floods and steams come against your life, you will remain immovable. The floods could be inflation, high prices, sickness, or any other problem. But God's promise is: No weapon formed against you will prosper. (Isa. 54:17.)

God's Word is eternal. If you plant incorruptible seed in your heart and do the things Jesus said, you will not fail!

Act on the Whole Word

In order to act on all of the principles, you may have to do a few things you don't want to do, such as praying for your enemies. (Luke 6:28.) If your enemies are hungry, feed them; if they are thirsty, give them a drink. (Rom. 12:20.)

If we begin to pray for our enemies, it won't be long before we won't have any! *When a man's ways please the Lord he maketh even his enemies to be at peace with him* (Prov. 16:7).

The man who built his house on the earth was trying to work on the surface. Many people try to use the Word as a formula without digging into the principles. The wise man dug deep to lay the foundation. You need to dig in the Word of God to find the principles and do the whole Word.

Dig a Deep Foundation

The man who builds his house on his confession only will get washed away. But the man who digs deep and lays the foundation on what Jesus said will remain. This man takes the time to find how the Kingdom works. He knows that it has to work because God's power and Word are behind it. He will be able to stand on it and believe it when the flood comes.

When the flood comes, the doer of the Word will stand, and the other man will pass away. People seeing the other man's house floating downstream may say, "He believed and he got washed away!" But they didn't know all the circumstances. He was washed away because he didn't dig deep and lay the foundation. The foundation is *doing* the Word.

Trials Come from the Devil

Some people believe that the storms and troubles of life come from the Lord to make us stronger. Luke 8 gives a classic example of why that can't be. Beginning in verse 22 it says:

Now it came to pass on a certain day, that he went into a ship with his disciples: and he said unto them, Let us go over unto the other side of the lake. And they launched forth.

But as they sailed he fell asleep: and there came down a storm of wind on the lake; and they were filled with water, and were in jeopardy.

And they came to him, and awoke him, saying, Master, master, we perish.

Jesus didn't say they were going to perish. He said, "We are going to the other side of the lake."

The disciples had let the Word depart from them. Satan stole the Word right out from under their nose!

What did Jesus do?

...He arose, and rebuked the wind and the raging of the water: and they ceased, and there was a calm.

And he said unto them, Where is your faith?

Their faith left on the wings of unbelief when they said, "We're going to drown!" They came to Jesus and told Him what the Devil said!

First John 3:8 gives the reason Jesus came to earth: *For this purpose the Son of God was manifested, that he might destroy the works of the devil. The Amplified Bible* says that he might "undo (destroy, loosen and dissolve)" the works that the Devil has done. Jesus stood in the bow of the boat and destroyed the storm with His Word. Did the Devil send the storm, or did God send the storm to perfect their faith?

The storm didn't *perfect* their faith; it *stole* their faith! Jesus said, "What did you do with your faith?" The Devil stole their faith because they let his words get into their mouths.

Jesus spoke to the wind and stopped it; He spoke to the sea and stopped the waves. *If the storm was from the Father, Jesus was destroying the works of His Father.* But we know He didn't destroy the works of His Father.

If it were true that trials and financial troubles are sent to make us stronger, Luke 6:48 would read this way:

"The man who heareth My sayings and doeth them is like unto a man that built his house on the sand. And when the stream beat upon it, and the trials came against it, and the flood arose against it, the windows broke, the roof blew off, and part of the siding came off; but, finally, the storm blew the house into the air, just high enough until a firm concrete foundation formed under it. And when the storm was over, his house was stronger."

This paraphrase is a little ridiculous, but it reveals the error of that kind of thinking. If trials and troubles of life were to perfect us, Jesus would have said every time a storm is through blowing and a stream is through beating, your house will be stronger.

Satan doesn't come to make you stronger or to help your faith. In the fourth chapter of Mark, Jesus said that Satan came to steal the Word of God. Satan may be able to steal the Word from some people; but if your foundation is firm, he won't be able to steal it from you!

The foundation is doing the sayings of Jesus—not being saved, or being filled with the Holy Ghost, or going to church, or paying your tithes; although these things are important. *Doing what Jesus said to do is what builds the foundation!*

You Must Sow the Seed

The psalmist David said, *I had fainted, unless I had believed to see the goodness of the Lord in the land of the living* (Ps. 27:13).

He is saying, "I would have fainted unless I could have seen God's goodness manifest here in this life, instead of just when I get to heaven."

Paul made this statement: *If in this life only we have hope in Christ, we are of all men most miserable* (1 Cor. 15:19). If our only hope was in this life, we *would* be miserable. However, if our only hope was when we get to heaven, we again would be miserable.

Jesus gives us the key to understanding how to operate in the Kingdom of God (how to receive God's blessings) when He says in Mark 4:14, *The sower soweth the word.*

If you have been saying, "I've just left it all up to God!" you haven't left it up to God. What you have done is to open the door to the Devil! Then whatever Satan does, you will think it was God doing it. God will not assume your responsibility. **You must act on Jesus' words.**

Yet a little sleep, a little slumber, a little folding of the hands to sleep:

So shall thy poverty come as one that travelleth, and thy want as an armed man.

Proverbs 6:10,11

If you fold your hands and say, "Lord, do whatever Your will is; I'm going to leave it all in Your hands," poverty will come as *one that travelleth*—as a roadrunner. You are, in essence, doing nothing!

It's dangerous for you to say, "Lord, just whatever You will, let it come to me." Whatever bad things the Devil brings your way, you will then accept as being the will of God. To pray specifically and accurately, you need to know the will or the Word of God; otherwise, you can open the door to tragedy and circumstances that will destroy you.

Resist the Devil! If you don't, God won't. God will allow anything you allow.

Find the will of God; then make your stand on it and proclaim it. Get knowledgeable in the Word, then *you* speak to the situation. What you speak will determine to a great degree what will happen. But it is you, *not God,* who must be motivated to act.

Speak to the Problem

And the Lord said, If ye had faith as a grain of mustard seed, ye might say unto this sycamine tree, Be thou plucked up by the root and be thou planted in the sea; and it should obey you.

Luke 17:6

The sycamine tree in this scripture is the problem, the circumstance, the situation that stands between you and your destination.

Jesus and the apostles were probably walking down a trail or a pathway and came upon a sycamine tree in the middle of the trail. It was an obstacle before them which they had to deal with in some way. Jesus used it as an object lesson.

He did not say, "If you had faith as a seed you would pray that God would move that obstacle before you. Then if you pray and cry and beg long enough, if you promise to be good and pay your tithes, then God will pluck it up for you and cast it into the sea."

No, He said, "Speak to it, and it will obey *you.*"

The *King James Version* says, "You *might* say to the tree...." The Greek New Testament says, "You *would* say." A stronger word is used in the Greek version, and it is the more accurate rendering in this instance. If you had faith as a seed, Jesus said you *would* speak to that sycamine tree (to that obstacle, that problem, that difficulty, that financial crisis you have been begging God to do something about). So quit begging and crying, and speak to that thing. Say what you want done with it. Tell it to be plucked up by the root!

Jesus said it would obey you!

There is no great theological reason why Jesus said to speak to the tree; He simply said to do it! He is telling you exactly how to get the Kingdom principles to work for you. Your voice is the voice of authority in your part of the earth. Whatever you bind will be bound. Whatever you loose will be loosed. The power of binding and loosing is on earth. It is a Kingdom principle. (Matt. 16:17-19.)

Speak Your Desire

Since every word that comes out your mouth is a potential seed and can be either a bad seed or a good seed, practice speaking only what God says, and only what you desire to come to pass. You will develop a habit in your spirit of releasing faith in every word you speak.

Continue Speaking the Solution

Several years ago I began to say that every disease germ and every virus that touches my body dies instantly, that I was redeemed from the curse of the Law, and that I forbade sickness and disease to operate in my body.

Though I said these things, I really didn't believe these statements were true in me. I knew the words were true. The Word of God said they would be true if I could get them in my heart; but I was saying them to get them into my heart. As David said, my tongue is as the pen of a ready writer. (Ps. 45:1.) Your tongue will write God's Word on the table of your heart.

When I got sick, someone said, "It didn't work, did it?" I said, "Yes! It's working. Faith is coming." I just kept saying it.

There's a difference between being a doer and "a tryer." If I had been "a tryer" of the Word, I would have given up the first time I was sick.

I wasn't *trying* the Word; I had set out to *do* the Word! I knew it would work! Jesus said it would. You can always find some "unbelieving believers," who don't believe the Word will work.

Jesus said, *All things are possible to him that believeth.* Are you a *him that believeth?*

When you say you are healed before the circumstances look that way, some people say you are lying. But if you study the Bible from Genesis to Revelation, you will discover that God called things that were not as though they were— and He expects us to do the same thing.

David Defeated the Devil in the Giant

We see in chapter 17 of 1 Samuel that David told the Philistine giant what he was going to do to him five times before he did it! He was using the principle of Matthew 17:20: *If ye have faith as a grain of mustard seed, ye shall say to this mountain, Remove hence to yonder place; and it shall remove.*

You can be sure of one thing: That giant looked like a mountain to David, who was only a 17-year-old boy. But David said boldly, ...*who is this uncircumcised Philistine, that he should defy the armies of the living God?* (1 Sam. 17:26). Then he went after him without even a sword in his hand. The only sword he had was the one in his mouth! (Rev. 2:16.) David killed the giant by speaking his faith.

When things look bad, continue to sow seed. Believe the best of the situation. Then if things grow worse and it looks like everything is against you, just keep your mouth shut. Don't speak negative words. Rest in what you have already established by your words.

You see, your words set the cornerstones of your life. Your faith is not always the same every day. There are times when you have the faith to believe the things you speak. The Word level is high. You have been meditating the Word. You believe what you say will come to pass. Then there are days which seem like all hell has broken loose. Nothing is working out and you feel like everything and everybody is against you. Though you made such great faith statements when your faith was high, it seems now that it will never come to pass.

Those are the days that you need to put a zipper on your lip! Don't say anything at all. Don't even try to make a faith confession when your faith is low, because most of the time it will be done out of fear in that situation.

Jairus Spoke the Solution

In the fifth chapter of Mark, we read a story, beginning in verse 22:

> *And, behold, there cometh one of the rulers of the synagogue, Jairus by name; and when he saw him (Jesus), he fell at his feet, and besought him greatly, saying,*
>
> *My little daughter lieth at the point of death: I pray thee, come and lay thy hands on her, that she may be healed; and she shall live.*
>
> *And Jesus went with him; and much people followed him, and thronged him.*

Here, Jairus has made a great faith statement. His daughter is not dead, but she is at the point of death. Jairus establishes that when Jesus lays His hands on his daughter, she shall be healed and she shall live. He established this by his faith-filled words. It is this faith which caused Jesus to leave the multitude and follow Jairus.

But on the way, a woman with an issue of blood comes on the scene. She touches Jesus' garment, receives her healing, then gives her testimony. All this could have taken an hour. Meanwhile, Jairus is still waiting for Jesus to heal his daughter. There has been a delay—a costly delay—and I'm sure that Jairus was getting quite anxious!

Then Jesus explains to the woman that it was her faith which made her whole. Verse 35 says: *While he yet spake, there came from the ruler of the synagogue's house certain which said, Thy daughter is dead: why troublest thou the Master any further?*

Thy daughter is dead. The very thing that Jairus knew could happen had happened! It couldn't have been any worse. His daughter was dead! Regardless of all he had believed, regardless of all the faith statements and confessions he had made, he gets the bad news: "It's too late, Jairus. Your daughter is already dead. Don't trouble the Master any longer."

Though Jairus had spoken good things, bad things had come his way. Verse 36 says, *As soon as Jesus heard the word that was spoken, he saith unto the ruler of the synagogue, Be not afraid, only believe. Jairus was obedient to the instruction of Jesus.*

If Jairus had allowed fear to come and had spoken what was on his mind, he probably would have said, "Jesus, if You hadn't stopped to heal that woman, You would have been there in time to heal my daughter!" Jairus would have gotten into strife, and they would have held a funeral a few days later.

But notice that Jairus didn't speak a word. Not one word proceeded from his mouth. We can learn from this. When things go wrong, when it looks like it's not going to work, when your faith is low, when all hell has broken loose against you and against your confession of faith, **just zip your lip!**

That is not the time to try to make some faith confessions. It is the time to rest in what you have already said—the words you spoke a few days before when your faith was high, when your Word level was high, when it looked like it was impossible for you to doubt that what you were saying would come to pass.

When the pressure is on, when the trouble and bad news have come, when it looks like nothing will help, when it seems that all hope is lost—that is the time to exercise the vocabulary of silence. Speak nothing! More than likely, if you try to make a confession at that point, you will speak words of fear instead of faith.

Jairus, a few hours before, had his mouth filled with the solution—the answer to his problem. He had established it in faith. But by this time, if he had asked somebody, "What will I do now? What's your opinion of this situation?" they would surely have told him, "It's too late, Jairus. Forget it! You've lost the battle. It's all over!"

But, thank God, Jairus didn't ask for anyone's opinion. Anything that he spoke in his situation would have been to affirm the solution instead of the problem. But the people around him wouldn't have understood, so he chose to be silent.

The end result of the whole matter was that his daughter was raised to life again. The words Jairus established in the beginning were fulfilled to the very letter!

When you speak the solution, calling those things that are not as though they were, people in the world won't understand. Just keep your eyes on Jesus, not on people's opinions. Disregard people's opinions and continue to speak the solution.

Let All Your Words Be Acceptable

Speak to the problem in prayer and in your conversations with other people.

Develop yourself to the point that you don't let negativism come out your mouth. Start believing that *every* word you say will come to pass.

Since you have a choice, why not say the good things instead of the bad? When you see a child run into a busy street after a ball, don't prophesy evil: "That kid's going to get run over. Just watch and see!" Instead, say: "In the name of Jesus, that child will not be hurt!"

Release your faith on the positive side of life.

Changing the Image

The fifth chapter of Mark describes a woman who had a negative image. The way she changed her image is a classic example of speaking the answer to the problem until the problem vanished.

And a certain woman, which had an issue of blood twelve years, and had suffered many things of many physicians, and had spent all that she had, and was nothing bettered, but rather grew worse,

When she had heard of Jesus, came in the press behind, and touched his garment. For she said, If I may touch but his clothes, I shall be whole.

And straightway the fountain of her blood was dried up; and she felt in her body that she was healed of that plague.

And Jesus, immediately knowing in himself that virtue had gone out of him, turned him about in the press, and said, Who touched my clothes?

And his disciples said unto him, Thou seest the multitude thronging thee, and sayest thou, Who touched me?

And he looked round about to see her that had done this thing.

But the woman fearing and trembling, knowing what was done in her, came and fell down before him, and told him all the truth.

And he said unto her, Daughter, thy faith hath made thee whole; go in peace, and be whole of thy plague.

Grow-Worse Image

This woman might have been rich when she started trying to get rid of her condition, but the Bible says she *had spent all that she had.*

After twelve years of getting progressively worse, spending money on doctors who could find no cure, she had developed a *grow-worse image.*

This woman believed what she heard about Jesus. Evidently she had heard that Jesus was healing people. God had told the children of Israel to sew a hem around the border of their garments as a symbol of the Covenant they had with Him. (Num. 15:38.) This woman was reaching out for that hem as she said, "When I touch His clothes, I'll be restored to health." You can see her faith in action.

The Amplified Bible says, "She *kept saying* when I touch his clothes, I *will* be whole." (v. 28.) What was she doing? She was speaking the solution rather than the problem. She was speaking words and changing her image inside.

To move from poverty to prosperity, or from sickness to health, you must first change your inner image. You may use the Word, medicine, or another method, but in order to receive whatever you desire, you must first change your image.

Divine healing is a spiritual cure. Your spirit changes the image on the inside. ***The woman with the issue of blood changed her image with the God-given plan of speaking what she desired with the words of her mouth.***

You may have tried everything you knew to make your business succeed to no avail. Within these pages, you have heard about Jesus and that His Kingdom is within you. If you take hold of the principles of the Kingdom and apply them, the *grow-worse image* inside you will change and you will have a success image.

A Positive Image

If you have had sickness and disease in your life for years, it may take a while for the image to change. Results won't come overnight, but a positive image will begin to form inside you if you will speak God's Word.

You can't expect to walk in prosperity and health if you talk poverty and sickness. Confession of God's Word keeps His answer before you. It will become a point of contact to change your image when you confess what God said; you'll begin to see a new image.

In the world system, salesmen go through training sessions to develop a positive self-image. A salesman will never rise above his self-image. If he sees himself a $200,000-insurance salesman, he will sell $200,000 worth of insurance wherever he is. If you put him in a position where he should sell $3,000,000 or where he should sell $10,000, he will still sell $200,000.

If you will get the image of God's Word within you, you will raise your sights. You will begin to talk wealth, life, and healing—instead of poverty, sickness, and death.

Don't talk about *my* sickness or *my* heart attack because they are the Devil's, not yours. Don't claim them! They will cause you to have a grow-worse image. Keep the answer before you.

Don't dwell on how your uncle died with some disease or how he was crippled in a car wreck. If you think continually about such bad things, they will fasten their laws upon you. You will draw them like a magnet. The more you talk about them, the more you will believe in them rather than life and health.

Talk instead about how your heavenly Father redeemed you from the curse of the Law, how He delivered you from the powers of darkness, and how you are healed by His stripes. Talk about how Jesus was made poor that you might be made rich, how God will supply abundantly if you will give and put the laws of prosperity to work.

Use God's Word as your point of contact to change your image. Release your faith as the Word of God changes the image inside you. Talk about the Word and think about it. If you sow the right kind of seed, you will reap the right kind of harvest. Get the image formed inside you, and eventually you will walk in health and prosperity. This is a principle of the Kingdom.

Words Created Everything

Genesis 1:1 says, *In the beginning God created the heaven and the earth.*

John 1:1-3 says, *In the beginning was the Word and the Word was with God, and the Word was God...All things were made by him;* (By whom? By the Word!) *and without him* [the Word] *was not any thing made that was made.*

Faith-filled words created everything; so if faith-filled words created everything, then faith-filled words can get rid of it or rearrange it.

Jesus Cursed the Fig Tree

In Luke 17:6, Jesus establishes the fact that inanimate objects will obey words:

> *If ye had faith as a grain of mustard seed, ye might say unto this sycamine tree, Be thou plucked up by the root, and be thou planted in the sea; and it should obey you.*

Jesus proves this principle by killing a fig tree with negative words. (Mark 11:20-23.) He cursed it, and the very next day it had dried up from the roots.

There are many people cursing their own "fig trees" without realizing it. When they say, "We can never afford the things we need," they are cursing their own fig tree; and if they continue, their finances will dry up! It will obey them because of the authority in their words—whether they are faith-filled words or fear-filled words. Both faith and fear are spiritual forces. Faith builds and fear destroys.

The mountain, the sycamine tree, or the fig tree in your life may be a physical condition for which you need healing, such as a tumor in your body.

You can speak to your body, and it will obey—if you believe and do not doubt *in your heart*. But it has to be an operation of the spirit, not just speaking out of your head.

To develop faith in your words, you must spend time. It doesn't come overnight. Faith comes by hearing the Word of God, so the speaking of God's Word is the way you develop faith in God's Word.

Speaking in line with God's Word will cause you to develop faith *in your words*. This is *the way* of life. It's not a fad. It's not something you use once in a while to get out of trouble. It's a principle of faith that Jesus taught and operated in throughout His ministry.

Jesus taught this principle: "Whosoever shall say to the mountain," and "If you had faith as a seed, you would say to the sycamine tree...." The conclusion of all His teaching is that **it would obey you!**

But the key to all of it is *believing that what you say will come to pass*—not just what you said to the mountain, not just what you said to the sycamine tree, but all the words you speak daily. In other words, you must *have faith in your words* and *speak them with authority and faith*. Then your words become spirit life.

It takes time to develop yourself in these Kingdom principles. Success in these principles do not come overnight. It takes weeks and months, sometimes even years, of diligent practice to get highly developed in believing that what you say will come to pass.

If you will spend the time and be diligent to practice your faith, to practice the Kingdom principles, the rewards are great. At this point, I want to share with you some illustrations of *speaking to things.*

Several years ago before I quit farming, I had planted my rice and it had rained and turned cold for several days. Neither the soil nor the temperature was conducive to sprouting seeds. So I was walking over my rice field, digging here and there to see what was happening to the rice I had sown. It showed very little sign of coming up.

I discovered that though some of the seed had soured, some was still good. I said to the Lord, "What am I going to do with this rice field? Do I need to plant it over?"

Proverbs states that when you have the Word in your heart, it will talk with you. (Prov. 6:22.) When you fill your heart by speaking God's words, your spirit can bring that Word up for use at any time. *The Word talks to you!* The Spirit of God rose up in me and said, "Why don't you do what the Word says? Speak to the problem. Speak to the rice and tell it what to do."

I thought, *Talk to my rice? You mean me?* Then I realized that I was not doing what I knew to do. I had the solution all the time, but had not acted.

So I walked around the rice field, pointed at the rice seed, and said, "In the name of Jesus, I am talking to you, *rice.* Listen to me. Sprout and come forth. Bring forth an abundant harvest." I suppose I spent an hour walking over that muddy field, talking to my seed.

Somebody may say, "That's ridiculous! I don't understand how that could work."

Actually, I didn't understand it either, but Jesus said, *Do it!* At times, you may appear ridiculous doing what Jesus says to do; but if you don't, you fail. Are you tired of failing? Jesus gave us the cure for failure: *Do His sayings.*

I spoke to the rice. It obeyed me. There was a beautiful harvest. I spoke to another field that had been planted two weeks earlier, but it didn't respond. When I asked the Lord why, He said that I waited too long—the seed was already ruined when I spoke to it. God's Word didn't fail; *I* failed.

Wheat Crop Obeys Words

One year my wheat crop looked so thin I wanted to plow it up for weeks; but the field stayed so wet that I couldn't get a tractor in it. Then my wife, Peggy, suggested that we confess God's Word over the wheat. I told her there just wasn't enough to leave, but she wouldn't give up. So I agreed to talk to it and confess God's Word over it.

In Matthew 18:19 Jesus said, *If two of you shall agree on earth as touching any thing that they shall ask, it shall be done for them of my Father which is in heaven.* So Peggy and I agreed, commanding the wheat to multiply, produce, and bring forth abundance.

You might say I took my Bible and sprayed the crop with Malachi 3:10-11. I read the Bible to my wheat, then said: "My ground is blessed! Insects will not devour it! The wheat will not cast its fruit before its time in the field, and *it is blessed of God!*"

That fall we cut 55 bushels per acre from the same field I wanted to plow up!

Housing Project Obeys Words

I had started developing a housing project near the town where we live, but the teaching ministry required so much of my time, I wasn't able to handle all the details. So I decided to sell the project and put more time into the ministry.

There were two houses in the project that hadn't sold. I said, "Lord, I prayed and I believed. Why haven't those houses sold?"

His answer was similar to the one concerning rice fields. He said, "Why don't you do what you've been teaching? Speak to the mountain."

Even though I knew this Bible principle well and had taught it many times, I had not acted on it in this situation. So I drove out to the project, walked up to one of the houses, and said: "House, listen to me: I'm talking to you, and I'm telling you to sell! Someone is impressed with you. I call you, *Sold!* Jesus said you would obey me." I felt silly, but I didn't let my feelings stop me. I walked inside and said the same things to the walls. Then I went to the other house and talked to it.

About a week later, my head (natural mind) began to give me trouble. It seemed to say, "Now, Big Mouth, what are you going to do?"

I remembered that the Lord had said in one of our meetings: *Tears of self-pity and sorrow do not release faith. Learn to release your faith in laughter.*

So, I drove to the project, stopped in front of each house, stuck my head out the window, and just laughed at the houses and the Devil.

There were mortgages that had accumulated on the housing project for water lines, sewer, etc., so I put these notes (totaling over $100,000) on the table and called in my daughter, Annette, as a witness to what I was doing. I pointed my finger at those mortgages and said:

"Listen to me, I'm talking to you! Be paid, in the name of Jesus. Disappear. Dematerialize. I don't care how you do it, but be gone! Be paid in full! Jesus said you would obey me."

Two weeks later the houses sold. A few weeks later the project sold, and the land behind the development sold. The notes were paid. The houses obeyed. The land obeyed. All of them obeyed faith-filled words.

Someone may say, "I tried it and it didn't work for me." That's very possible because it won't work if you just *try it.* You must be a doer of the Word. Apply the principles of the Kingdom and spend the time to develop your words. It won't work just because you say it, but saying it is involved in working the principle of faith. It takes weeks and months of being diligent in speaking God's promises to develop your faith to believe that what you say will come to pass.

The House in Minnesota

During a meeting in Minneapolis when I was sharing these experiences, a lady came to me after the service and said, "Glory to God! Now I know how to sell my house. I'm going to talk to it right now! And when it sells, I'm going to give the tithes into your ministry."

Within three weeks she sold her house. It had been on the market for several months, but it sold when she spoke to it. It obeyed her words.

If you diligently do what Jesus said, these principles will work in your life. But you must come to Jesus, hear His sayings, then do them.

Are you willing to do what Jesus said, even to the point of appearing ridiculous to the world?

Some may say, "The rice fields, the wheat crop, the housing project, and the house in Minnesota are just a coincidence!"

But the Word worked for Jesus, and He said, "If you do My sayings, you won't fail."

The harvest produced by the seeds that *your voice* plants will cause the sycamine tree to remove or to remain. **But it will** obey you.

Things To Remember

Do the sayings of Jesus and you will have
a house with a firm foundation.
The floods and storms of life do not come from God.

Plant God's Word in your heart and do the
sayings of Jesus, and you will not fail.

Dig in the Word to find the principles,
then do the whole Word.

You must do God's Word yourself; God won't do it for you!

Speak God's Word to the problem in your life.
Practice speaking what God says about you.
Develop the habit of releasing faith in every word you speak.

Start believing that *every* word you say will come to pass.

Confessing God's Word forms a positive image inside you.

The image of God's Word will raise your sights.

God's Word is your point of contact to change your image.

Speaking in line with God's Word will
cause you to develop faith in *your* words.
The key is believing what you say will come to pass.

For these principles to work in your life,
you must come to Jesus, hear His sayings,
then diligently do what He says.

13

Using the Faith You Have

When the disciples became afraid in midst of a storm, Jesus asked them, *Where is your faith?* (Luke 8:22-27).

Jesus later spoke to them and said, *O ye of little faith...* (Luke 12:28). They didn't like that, so they decided to ask Him to give them *more* faith. Luke 17:5 says, *The apostles said unto the Lord, Increase our faith.*

The apostles couldn't read Mark 4 or 11:23-24 to find out how the Kingdom of God operates.

Then again in Matthew 17 the disciples failed to cast a demon out of a boy, so Jesus had to cast it out. Later when Jesus was alone with them, they asked Him why they couldn't do it.

And Jesus said unto them, Because of unbelief: for verily I say unto you, If ye have faith as a grain of mustard seed, ye shall say unto this mountain, Remove hence to yonder place; and it shall remove; and nothing shall be impossible unto you (v. 20).

These words are similar to what Jesus said in Luke 17:6: *If ye had faith as a grain of mustard seed, ye might say unto this sycamine tree, Be thou plucked up....*

Both of these examples—the mountain in Matthew 17:20 and the sycamine tree in Luke 17:6—refer to the problem, to the circumstance before them.

Jesus did not say, "If you have faith the size of a seed...," but, "If you have faith as a grain of mustard seed...." Jesus is using as an example a type of seed that is familiar to the apostles. (Had Jesus been in England, Arkansas, He would have said, "If you had faith as a cotton seed....")

The size of the seed doesn't matter. The point is that the seed is good for only one thing: to plant.

Jesus is saying you don't need more faith, but you must be willing to plant it, to put it to work, to say to the problem, "Be removed!"

In answer to the apostles' request to give them more faith, Jesus said, "You don't need more faith. You just need to use the faith you have by speaking it."

Plant your Faith

Luke 17:6 and Matthew 17:20 contain three great secrets of faith:

1. Faith works like a seed.

2. You must plant it to get the benefit of that faith seed.

3. You plant faith by speaking it.

The Kingdom operates by the principle of sowing and reaping: *...as a man should cast seed into the ground* (Mark 4:26).

From studying the teachings of Jesus, Peter, James, and others, I believe seeds cannot be planted in your heart unless you first speak words. They will never get in there unless you speak them there. They are in the mouth first, then in the heart. (Rom. 10:8.)

Leave Your Seed in the Ground

There is something you should remember when planting seeds of faith: Once the seed is planted, you no longer have it; it's in the ground (heart).

Often people use the phrase, "I'm believing for..." (I have said it myself.) But if you are *believing for it,* you are in the process; but you haven't believed yet. Once you have believed it, it is settled!

Once the seed is planted, you don't go back to dig it up! It is the substance of what you desire. Praise God for it, even though it's not in your possession, because *you have believed!* Past tense! You shall receive.

If you say, *"I am believing* for this," you are in the process of believing; but when you say, *"I have believed* God for it," then it is settled! The seed is planted. You no longer have it. You've traded faith for the thing you believed.

When you go to the store, you gather your groceries, then take them to the cash register. The cashier tells you the amount of the groceries, and you lay your money on the counter. After your groceries are bagged, if you pick up both your money and the groceries and start out the door, the cashier will say, "Wait a minute! You have to leave one of them here, either the groceries or the money. You can't leave with both!"

When you believed, you settled it! You planted your faith. Don't dig it up, because you can't have both the seed and the harvest. You have already believed. Leave your faith and confess the harvest.

Let's look at the conversation between Jesus and the centurion:

> *The centurion said, Lord, my servant lieth at home sick of the palsy, grievously tormented.*
>
> *And Jesus saith unto him, I will come and heal him.*
>
> *The centurion answered and said, Lord, I am not worthy that thou shouldest come under my roof: but speak the word only, and my servant shall be healed.*
>
> *For I am a man under authority, having soldiers under me: and I say to this man, Go, and he goeth; and to another, Come, and he cometh; and to my servant, Do this, and he doeth it.*
>
> Matthew 8:6-9

When Jesus heard these words, He stopped and preached a sermon.

When Jesus heard it, he marvelled, and said to them that followed, Verily I say unto you, I have not found so great faith, no, not in Israel (v. 10).

This centurion was a Gentile, a Roman. He was not under the Covenant that God had with Israel; yet Jesus said his was the greatest faith He had seen in all Israel!

Then Jesus said, *Go thy way; and as thou hast believed* (past tense), *so be it done unto thee. And his servant was healed in the selfsame hour* (v. 13).

The centurion released his faith when he said to Jesus, *Speak the word only, and my servant shall be healed.* He was not believing; he had *already* believed. He planted the seed and left it in the ground. Jesus said to him, *As thou hast believed* (not "As you are believing"), *so be it done unto thee.*

Words Are Your Servants

But which of you, having a servant plowing or feeding cattle, will say unto him by and by, when he is come from the field, Go and sit down to meat?

And will not rather say unto him, Make ready wherewith I may sup, and gird thyself, and serve me, till I have eaten and drunken; and afterward thou shalt eat and drink?

Doth he thank that servant because he did the things that were commanded him? I trow not.

Luke 17:7-9

You can state the point of the above passage in two different ways: Faith is the servant of the believer, or faith-filled words are the servant of the believer. Actually you can say it three ways:

The sycamine tree obeys **you.**

The sycamine tree obeys **your words.**

The sycamine tree obeys **your faith.**

In Bible days, no master had his servant rest or eat before serving him.

As soon as the servant came in from plowing or feeding cattle, he cooked the meal and fed the master; then he ate the leftovers later.

Don't Relax After Victory

Faith-filled words become your servants, working for you day in and day out. When they bring in the victory, you don't say to your words: "Since you won that victory, I'm going to let you relax a few days." When they are through with one job, don't let them lie around and get lazy. After spending a long day working, the servant in Luke 17 came home to do more work.

Again, I refer to Matthew 12:36 in which Jesus said we will give an account of every idle word spoken. If you let your servant—faith-filled words—lie around idle, you will give an account of them.

As the master kept the servant working in Luke 17, we must keep our words working. We do that by speaking the thing desired—giving them a new assignment.

Things To Remember

Learn to use your faith as a seed.

Plant your faith by speaking it.

Once the seed is planted, don't dig it up.

Faith-filled words are your servants.

They work for you day and night.

Keep your words working!

14

Faith Is Not Laziness

You must hear God's Word intelligently, then put some action to your faith.

Several years ago there was a couple in a city where I was teaching on a weekly basis who took hold of the faith and confession message. They had moved to that city because the man had taken a new job there, but the company he was to work for went broke about the time he and his wife arrived. They were living in a very expensive apartment, and since neither of them had a job, bills began to pile up.

They learned a part of what they heard about confession, but they only got the formula. They thought all they had to do was say it. So they sat at home confessing that they had the money to meet their bills.

The man was offered a job selling cars for $600 a month, plus commission, but he turned it down. He said he was "waiting for his ship to come in." (One thing should be clear: If you haven't sent one out, it won't come in!) The Word says, *...whatsoever he doeth shall prosper* (Ps. 1:3). This man wasn't *doing* anything, and a hundredfold return on *nothing* is still *nothing!*

Confession didn't work for the couple who only sat around confessing. They didn't have the principle of seedtime and harvest. They didn't use common sense, and they weren't being obedient to God's Word, which says, ...*whatsoever he doeth shall prosper.* They weren't doing anything. Confession and faith are powerful when coupled with doing the Word of God.

Sometimes people miss it in the walk of faith. They get "turned on" to faith and say, "Glory to God! I'm going to quit my job!" Let me share a few words of wisdom: If you can't make it by faith *with* a job, you certainly won't make it by faith *without* a job.

Use Common Sense

Some people act on the Word but miss God by trying to substitute faith for good business practices. When they hear about faith principles and learn the importance of confession, they go off on a tangent, throwing away all common sense and good business practices.

One time someone asked me, "Brother Capps, do you use fertilizer on your farm?"

In response, I asked him, "Do you use gas in your car?"

Some people seem to throw away all common sense when they start using their faith.

Somebody may say, "Instead of advertising, I'm just going to believe God." If God tells you to do that, fine; but just be sure God said it.

Don't substitute faith for good business practices.

Don't substitute good business practices for faith.

You have to put the two together. Use faith in all your business practices. When you start saying good things about your work, the results will astound you.

Follow Instructions

Let me give you an example of how to act on the Word to sow the seed.

The Lord might instruct you to give $50 to a particular person. The Word of God concerning giving in Luke 6:38 says, *Give, and it shall be given unto you; good measure, pressed down, and shaken together, and running over.* In order to sow the seed, you must do what this verse says. Luke 6:38 will not work unless you observe the principles of the laws of prosperity. You can't just *know* what the Word says about giving; you must give in order to claim this promise.

Give, and it shall be given. The phrase *shall be* is future tense. The promise is before you. It doesn't belong to you until you do what God's Word says.

The instant you give that $50, you can speak that promise into your heart because you have been obedient to God. Instead of saying, "It *shall* be given unto me," you can say, "Father, Your Word says, *Give, and it shall be given.* Then because I have given, *it is given unto me—good measure, pressed down, and shaken together, and running over.*"

That is present tense: It **is** given **now!** Before you obeyed, the return from giving was *shall be.* After you obeyed by giving, your confession changed to *it is given to me.*

Say Before You See

Once you have acted, you can take God's Word and put it in the present tense: "Father, because I have given, it is given unto me—*good measure, pressed down, and shaken together, and running over.*"

Someone may say, "You don't have it yet." But you don't have to see it. Trust God; He wouldn't lie to you!

Continue to sow the Word of God into your heart by your words. Say, "Thank You, Father, it is given unto me. I'm believing for a hundredfold return, in the name of Jesus, and it is coming to me. The blessings are overtaking me because I sow bountifully and I reap bountifully. I have all sufficiency in all things and do abound to every good work. The Lord is my Shepherd, and I do not want."

Speak the Words Aloud

As we have seen, the way you sow the Word of God is to hear your voice utter what God said. This is one of the keys to operating in God's Kingdom. You don't have to let your voice echo off the walls, but you do need to say your confessions aloud.

Paul said, *Faith cometh by hearing, and hearing by the word of God* (Rom. 10:17). The Greek for *word* in this verse is *rhema* or "the spoken Word." By *rhema of God,* Paul in this verse is referring to a portion of Scripture. He does not mean the whole Bible, or *logos.* I am convinced that Paul was saying, "Faith comes by hearing yourself speak God's Word."

This is God's principal way of causing faith to come. God uses it to transfer His faith to you, and it's done through His

Word. God's Word is filled with faith. Therefore, when you quote God's Word aloud, it imparts that faith to you. God has always used this basic principle. He used it when He made His Covenant with Abraham.

God Spoke—Abraham Quoted

In Genesis 17 God appeared to Abraham and said, "I have made thee the father of many nations." At that time, Abraham and Sarah didn't even have the promised child, but God said, "I have already done it!"

Then God proceeded to set in motion the principle of faith to cause it to come to pass. Abraham was 99 years old and his wife was 90, so there was no natural hope. But the Bible says when there was no hope, Abraham believed in hope. (Rom. 4:18.)

God set this plan in motion by changing Abram's name to Abraham and changing Sarai's name to Sarah. *Abraham* means "father of nations" or "father of a multitude." *Sarah* means "mother of nations" or "mother of a multitude." When God renamed them, He forced them into saying, "I am the father of nations" and "I am the mother of nations." God had set in motion His basic principles of transferring His faith to Abraham and Sarah, so that what He had promised would surely come to pass.

Every time Abraham said, "My name is Abraham," he was saying, "I am the father of nations." Every time Sarah said, "I am Sarah," she was saying, "I am the mother of nations" or "the mother of multitudes."

It was the speaking of God's Word which had been spoken to them that caused faith to come. Every time someone said, "Abraham, what are we to do now?" he didn't hear *Abraham,* he heard *Father of Nations.*

With all the people who worked for him, Abraham's name was probably called hundreds of times a day. Can you imagine what that did to his faith? He heard "Father of Nations...Father of Nations. O Father of Nations...." Day in and day out, he heard what God said.

Then in the same way, all the maids who called to Sarah called her, "Mother of Nations."

This was as if God had said, "Thus saith the Lord," because it was the Word of the Lord to Abraham and Sarah, and it caused faith to come—faith sufficient to cause the promise to come to pass.

This has always been God's method. It is still God's method today. Faith in God comes by hearing the Word of God. When God wants a harvest, He Himself plants a seed.

The Seed Has Always Existed

The Kingdom of God has always worked in the same way, by sowing seeds, because the Seed—the Word of God which is Jesus—has always existed, and always will.

As Genesis 3:15 shows, Jesus Christ is considered "the Seed." In this verse God said to the serpent, *I will put enmity between thee and the woman, and between thy seed and her seed; it shall bruise thy head, and thou shalt bruise his heel.*

The "seed" God is talking about is Jesus Christ. God made the promise of the Covenant to Abraham and his seed:

Now to Abraham and his seed were the promises made. He saith not, And to seeds, as of many; but as of one, And to thy seed, which is Christ (Gal. 3:16).

In Genesis 17:7 God said to Abraham, *I will establish my covenant between me and thee and thy seed after thee in their generations for an everlasting covenant.*

Jesus is the Seed; and since Jesus and the Word are one, the Seed is the Word of God. All through the Bible from Genesis to Revelation, you will find that the Word of God is considered to be the Seed.

According to 1 Peter 1:23, the Word of God lives forever: *Being born again, not of corruptible seed, but of incorruptible, by the word of God, which liveth and abideth for ever.*

According to John's Gospel, Jesus and the Word are one:

In the beginning was the Word, and the Word was with God, and the Word was God.

The same was in the beginning with God.

All things were made by him; and without him was not any thing made that was made...

And the Word was made flesh, and dwelt among us.

John 1:1-3,14

If in the beginning the Word was God, then the Word is still God over every situation of life.

Things To Remember

You must put some action to your faith:
Whatsoever he doeth shall prosper.

Confession and faith are powerful when
coupled with doing the Word of God.

Use common sense.

Don't substitute faith for good business practices.

Sow the Word of God into your heart.
Faith comes by hearing yourself speak God's Word.

15

Taking No Anxious Thought

A common enemy to success in any individual's life is fear—the fear of failure. Because of this fear, many people become anxious, fearful, overwrought, and distressed. But on almost every occasion when Jesus presented Himself to the disciples after He arose from the dead, His greeting was: *Fear not* or *Be not afraid.*

Even when Jesus spoke of all the things that were to come upon the earth, He said, *See that ye be not troubled* (Matt. 24:6). On other occasions He said, *Let not your heart be troubled* (John 14:27). In Matthew 6:25 Jesus admonishes us to take no anxious thought, but this is the first thing most people do concerning the things of their lives—finances, housing, and all the necessities of life.

Listen to the words of Jesus as He tells you a better way:

Therefore I say unto you, Take no thought for your life, what ye shall eat, or what ye shall drink; nor yet for your body, what ye shall put on. Is not the life more than meat, and the body than raiment?

Behold the fowls of the air: for they sow not, neither do they reap, nor gather into barns; yet your heavenly Father feedeth them. Are ye not much better than they?

Which of you by taking thought can add one cubit unto his stature? And why take ye thought for raiment?

Consider the lilies of the field, how they grow; they toil not, neither do they spin: and yet I say unto you, That even Solomon in all his glory was not arrayed like one of these.

Wherefore, if God so clothe the grass of the field, which to day is, and to morrow is cast into the oven, shall he not much more clothe you, O ye of little faith?

Therefore take no thought, saying, What shall we eat? or, What shall we drink? or, Wherewithal shall we be clothed? (For after all these things do the Gentiles seek:) for your heavenly Father knoweth that ye have need of all these things.

Matthew 6:25-32

Now notice verse 31: *Take no thought, saying....* It's all right to take thought. It's all right to make plans. But don't take thought by *saying,* "What am I going to do? Interest rates are 21 percent! Dear God, what are we going to do?" That will only produce fear, doubt, and unbelief. It will never produce faith. Faith comes by hearing God's Word.

If you must say something in this situation, go to the Word of God and say what the Apostle Paul said: *But my God shall supply all your need according to his riches in glory by Christ Jesus* (Phil. 4:19). In the place where it says, *your need,* just insert your name.

Jesus said, "Don't take thought by *saying.*" Words are the most powerful force in the universe. If they are used right, they will put you over in life. If they are used wrong, they will destroy your faith and put you down in life. Jesus is telling you something here that is very vital: **Don't take**

thought by *saying*. You may *think* those thoughts some-times, but don't *say* them.

You can't keep the Devil from putting doubt in your mind; but if you will refuse to speak it, it will die unborn. **Doubt will die unborn unless you speak it.** Once you speak it, you give birth to it. Then it becomes unbelief. So grit your teeth and keep your mouth shut. There is a time to speak and a time to be silent.

When your Word level is low and your faith is low, don't start trying to make a faith confession. You will be making your confessions in fear.

Confessions in Fear

You can get built up to the point where you confess the Word of God: "My God meets my need according to His riches in glory." You have prayed. You have confessed God's Word. You believe you have received. You have thanked God for it. There is no doubt in your mind at that point that you have received. You believe it with your heart.

But then five days later when it hasn't come to pass, the Devil comes along and everything seems to be going against you. You are on a low limb! That *is not* the time to start trying to make a confession of your faith! Just rest on what you said in faith five days before. It is possible to make right statements in fear.

As we have already seen from the fifth chapter of Mark, Jairus came to Jesus in faith. He said, *My little daughter lieth at the point of death: I pray thee, come and lay thy hands on her, that she may be healed; and she shall live*

(v. 23). Now that was a faith statement. Jairus spoke those words when his faith was high. He believed that Jesus could heal his daughter.

But later someone comes and says, "Jairus, your daughter is already dead. Just forget it. Don't trouble the Master anymore." Jairus had spoken in faith, but now the dry winds of doubt were blowing against him. He was in a bad situation. That was not the time for him to start making faith confessions. He just needed to rest on the statement he had made when his faith was high.

Don't misunderstand me. You *can* go to the Word of God and quote it in a situation like that, but there is a difference between making a confession of God's Word as an exercise of faith and doing it in fear. I have heard people say these things in fear. They were saying it, not because of the faith that was in their hearts, but because they were afraid that very thing was going to happen. They started making confessions in fear.

But Jairus just kept his mouth shut.

You can quote God's Word in this kind of situation; just quote it over and over to yourself. Then when you want to speak a word of faith to effect something, you will be filled with the Word of God. Your faith and your Word level will be high.

There is a difference between saying God's Word to put it inside you and speaking the Word out to effect something. There are times when all Christians have some doubt. Don't try to speak the word of faith at those times. Start speaking it to put it in your heart and cause faith to come; or, just keep your mouth shut as Jairus did.

Words Produce Faith or Fear

Jesus said, *Take no thought, **saying.*** Why should Jesus be concerned about our taking thought by *saying?* Because saying will produce either faith or fear.

Speak faith-filled words, and they will produce faith. Speak fear-filled words, and they will produce fear. I can say things to you that will produce a degree of faith in you; or, I can speak words that will create a sense of fear in you.

Statements like, "What are we going to do? How are we going to make this payment?" produce fear. When you fear, you allow Satan to steal the Word from you. Every time you say such things, you are opening the door for the Devil to speak to your carnal mind. You are to take no thought by saying anything that would open the door to the Devil.

The Devil clouding your mind with such thoughts is a major area you must deal with if you expect to walk in God's prosperity. Jesus told us to *take no thought by saying* because the human spirit is designed to produce in like kind from the seed you plant in your heart. If you plant thoughts based on worry, your spirit will produce—and, in fact, lead you to—the very thing you fear.

Remember this: *Satan is very limited in what he can do unless you fear!* Fear releases his ability against you. He can no more prevail against you if you are without fear than God can move in your behalf without faith! Faith brings God on the scene, but fear is an invitation to Satan.

Learn to control your vocabulary and harness your tongue, because by your words you release the ability of Satan against your finances, your home, and your physical body.

Things To Remember

Fear of failure is an enemy to success.

Resist fear as you would resist the Devil.

You can't keep the Devil from putting doubt in your mind; but if you refuse to speak it, the doubt will die unborn.

Faith-filled words produce faith;
fear-filled words produce fear.

Fear brings Satan on the scene.
Faith brings God on the scene.

16

Refusing Wisdom Produces Fear and Calamity

God's Word instructs us: *Wisdom is the principal thing; therefore get wisdom* (Prov. 4:7). Then it says that wisdom comes out of the mouth of God. (Prov. 2:6.)

Too often when people are caught up in problems, troubles, calamities, and failures, you will hear them say, "Why did God allow this to come? Why didn't God do something about this? Why did it have to happen to me?"

Well, let's go to the book of Proverbs and see what God's Word says about it.

Because I have called, and ye refused; I have stretched out my hand, and no man regarded;

But ye have set at nought all my counsel, and would none of my reproof:

I also will laugh at your calamity; will mock when your fear cometh;

When your fear cometh as desolation, and your destruction cometh as a whirlwind; when distress and anguish cometh upon you.

Then shall they call upon me, but I will not answer; they shall seek me early, but they shall not find me:

For that they hated knowledge, and did not choose the fear of the Lord:

They would none of my counsel: they despised all my reproof.

Therefore shall they eat of the fruit of their own way, and be filled with their own devices.

For the turning away of the simple shall slay them, and the prosperity of fools shall destroy them.

But whoso hearkeneth unto me (wisdom) shall dwell safely, and shall be quiet from fear of evil.

Proverbs 1:24-33

If you hearken unto wisdom, you will be quiet from fear of evil!

Turn at the reproof of wisdom, which is the Word of God *that they may recover themselves out of the snare of the devil* (2 Tim. 2:26). **You** have to recover **yourself** out of some things; God can't do it for you.

Fear-Enemy to Success

Job did not do all the things described in the above passage, but he did fear. (Even though a man walks upright before God, he can still miss God.) *For the thing which I greatly feared is come upon me* (Job 3:25). Job didn't just fear, he greatly feared!

Remember all the times Jesus said, "Fear not. Neither be afraid. Don't be afraid. Fear not!" He wasn't just making up scriptures to fill the Bible; He was revealing a secret: **Fear will produce the very thing you fear, the same as faith will produce the very thing you believe.** Jesus said,

"Don't take anxious thought," because it will dig up the Word that you've sown.

You can pray the most beautiful prayer, full of faith, then talk that seed right out of the ground!

Fear Draws Oppression

When you fear, the thing you are fearing will come upon you because fear is a spiritual force: *God hath not given us the spirit of fear; but of power, and of love, and of a sound mind* (2 Tim. 1:7).

Fear is a spirit that will draw the very thing you do not desire! In Isaiah 54:14 God told Israel, *...thou shalt be far from oppression; **for thou shalt not fear:** and from terror; for it* (fear) *shall not come near thee.*

Fear draws oppression. It draws all the negative forces.

When Job *greatly feared*, he set in motion the formula for failure. He said, *For the thing which I greatly feared is come upon me, and that which I was afraid of is come unto me. I was not in safety, neither had I rest, neither was I quiet; yet trouble came* (Job 3:25,26).

In the first chapter of Job, you will find that the indictment Satan brought against God was that He had put a hedge around Job. (v. 10.) Job was safe until he began to fear. He couldn't rest for fear of what was going to happen. He was actually calling things that were not, but he did it on the negative side. He continually offered sacrifices to God.

We have an advantage over Job because we can read the Book of Job and find out that Satan was the one who caused Job's trouble. Job thought God did it. He said, *...the Lord* *gave, and the Lord hath taken away; blessed be the name of the Lord* (Job 1:21).

This statement by Job is in the Bible, but is it the truth? As someone so aptly put it: It is a true statement of Job's opinion, but it is not a statement of truth. The Lord gave and the Devil took away.

God's Word Frees You From Fear

Proverbs 1:33 says, *But whoso hearkeneth unto me shall dwell safely, and shall be quiet from fear of evil.*

As we have already seen, *hearken* means "to declare," so this verse means, "Hearken unto Me—declare unto Me what I have said." Speaking words such as, "I am far from oppression!" will set forces at work for you to keep fear and other negative forces away from your life.

According to Proverbs 3, putting God's wisdom—the Word of God—into your heart will free you from fear:

> *My son, let not them (wisdom and knowledge) depart from thine eyes: keep sound wisdom and discretion: so shall they be life unto thy soul...*

> *Then shalt thou walk in thy way safely, and thy foot shall not stumble.*

> *When thou liest down, thou shalt not be afraid: yea, thou shalt lie down, and thy sleep shall be sweet.*

> *Be not afraid of sudden fear, neither of the desolation of the wicked, when it cometh. For the Lord shall be thy confidence, and shall keep thy foot from being taken.*

Proverbs 3:21-26

These words will do wonders for building up the soulish man, as well as the spirit, and free you from fear!

Some say, "You're just ignoring the problems." On the contrary, I'm doing something about them by planting seed in my heart that will overcome the problem.

Let's look at God's wisdom in Proverbs.

A man's heart deviseth his way: but the Lord directeth his steps.

Proverbs 16:9

The wise in heart shall be called prudent: and the sweetness of the lips increaseth learning.

Understanding is a wellspring of life unto him that hath it: but the instruction of fools is folly.

The heart of the wise teacheth his mouth, and addeth learning to his lips.

Pleasant words are as an honeycomb, sweet to the soul, and health to the bones.

There is a way that seemeth right unto a man, but the end thereof are the ways of death.

Proverbs 16:21-25

Again, verse 24 says, **Pleasant words** are as an honeycomb, sweet to the soul, and **health to the bones.**

To some people it seems right to say, "You just don't know how bad it is with me. You just don't know how the Devil is destroying my home. You just don't know how mean my husband is. You just don't know how poor we are. We can't afford things. If I ever get a job, I'll lose it."

There is a way that seems right to a man, but the end is going to destroy him. It seems right for somebody to say, "I'm not going to say I'm healed when I still hurt. If I was really healed, I wouldn't hurt." That may seem right to you, but the end result of it may kill you, especially if you are in the position where the doctors have given you up to die.

I am talking about an individual who has become so pious that he thinks he is lying if he doesn't say what already exists. The individual who continually says what is, is always establishing present circumstances.

To operate in Kingdom principles—*Whosoever shall say, believe, doubt not in his heart, but believe what he says will come to pass, he shall have whatsoever he says*—you must speak to the mountain, not *about* the mountain.

Some people wouldn't dare to speak to the mountain or speak to the sycamine tree. They wouldn't dare say that it is removed and cast into the sea. You have to learn to do what the Word says to do. This is the way God's Kingdom works.

Now let's look at some of the things Proverbs says about the tongue.

The fruit of the righteous is a tree of life.

Proverbs 11:30

The wicked is snared by the transgression of his lips: but the just shall come out of trouble.

A man shall be satisfied with good by the fruit of his mouth: and the recompence of a man's hands shall be rendered unto him.

Proverbs 12:13,14

There is that speaketh like the piercings of a sword: but the tongue of the wise is health.

Proverbs 13:18

A man shall eat good by the fruit of his mouth: but the soul of the transgressors shall eat violence.

He that keepeth his mouth keepeth his life: but he that openeth wide his lips shall have destruction.

Proverbs 13:2,3

The tongue of the wise useth knowledge aright: but the mouth of fools poureth out foolishness.

The eyes of the Lord are in every place, beholding the evil and the good.

A wholesome tongue is a tree of life: but perverseness therein is a breach in the spirit.

Proverbs 15:2-4

A wholesome tongue is the nearest thing we have to the tree of life that was in the Garden of Eden. You see, Adam could have eaten of the tree of life. He could have partaken of divine life provisions from that tree, but he didn't. He chose to eat of the knowledge of blessing and calamity.

The nearest thing to that today is the wholesome tongue. It becomes the tree of life to you, for with the tongue you sow seeds in the Kingdom. That's the way the Kingdom works.

Notice Proverbs 15:4 says, *...perverseness therein is a breach in the spirit.* Perverseness of the tongue will cause a broken spirit.

Proverbs 15:13 says, *A merry heart maketh a cheerful countenance: but by sorrow of the heart the spirit is broken.*

Proverbs 17:22 says, *A merry heart doeth good like a medicine: but a broken spirit drieth the bones.* Proverbs 15:23 tells us, *A man hath joy by the answer of his mouth.*

If you don't have joy, check up on your mouth!

Through desire a man, having separated himself, seeketh and intermeddleth with all wisdom (Prov. 18:1). You must separate yourself from some of the things of the world and intermeddle with the wisdom of God.

A fool's mouth is his destruction, and his lips are the snare of his soul (Prov. 18:7). A fool's mouth is his destruction. There is an old saying: "Sticks and stones may break my bones, but words will never hurt me." That's a lie! Wrong words kill you, especially if **you** speak them.

A man's belly [innermost being] *shall be satisfied with the fruit of his mouth...* (Prov. 18:20). What a person speaks out his mouth is what he will get in his heart. Your heart will be satisfied with it if you speak it—whether it is right, wrong, or indifferent. *...and with the increase of his lips shall he be filled.* You will be filled with the things you speak out your mouth.

Death and life are in the power of the tongue: and they that love it shall eat the fruit thereof (Prov. 18:21). You are going to eat the fruit of your mouth, either death or life.

Deposit God's Word in your heart by speaking it. *The righteousness which is of faith speaketh on this wise...The word is nigh thee, even in thy mouth and in thy heart* (Rom. 10:6,8).

God's Word will take care of inflation and recession if we are diligent to do what Jesus said—if we take no anxious thought by saying, "What am I going to do? What are we going to eat? What's going to happen to us?"

Program Yourself With the Word

You must fully program yourself with the Word of God until you no longer take anxious thought and become fretful over your needs. God takes care of the lilies of the field and the fowl of the air. Jesus said He would clothe even those who have just a little faith!

Sow the Word of God in your heart and act on the faith that you have. It doesn't take much faith, just faith as a seed.

Sowing seed for success is *our* responsibility. Seeing that the success comes to pass is *God's* responsibility—once we have done our part. We don't have to beg God for it to come to pass. The ground is designed to work.

In Mark 4:26-27 Jesus tells us that the Kingdom works as a man who casts seed in the ground, and then carries on life as usual *without worrying*. After planting their crops, farmers don't start praying that the ground will work!

Jesus said, *Take no thought, saying, What shall we eat? or, What shall we drink? or, Wherewithal shall we be clothed?* (Matt. 6:31). We don't have to take thought for these things because God is responsible for supplying our needs. All we do is sow the seed.

To keep from worrying, develop an unchanging trust in God.

People in the world have natural faith. As Christians, we have a different kind of faith, a level of faith not learned from books or from experiences, but from God's Word. This faith is based on a knowledge of God that He has created and developed within us. To build and strengthen this faith, to stay quiet from the fear of evil, you must learn to keep God's Word in your mouth.

Things To Remember

Fear is a spiritual force that draws all the negative forces.

Fear will produce the very thing you fear,
the same as faith will produce the very thing you believe.

Programming yourself with the Word of God
builds a resistance to the force of fear.

Whoso hearkeneth unto me (wisdom) *shall
dwell safely, and shall be quiet from fear of evil.*
By hearkening unto God's Wisdom—
His Word—you will have no fear of evil.

17

Reaping the Harvest

For the earth bringeth forth fruit of herself; first the blade, then the ear, after that the full corn in the ear.

Mark 4:28

It Takes Time for Faith To Develop

You must develop yourself in the Kingdom principles. As it takes time for seeds to grow, it also takes time for you to develop yourself to believe what you are saying will come to pass. You may start speaking to things, but that doesn't mean the things will obey you *immediately*.

The woman with the issue of blood described in the fifth chapter of Mark took four steps: speaking, acting, receiving, and knowing. Apparently this happened in a relatively short period of time; however, when you follow these steps, *results usually will not happen overnight.*

Before anything changes on the outside—before you feel better or look better—the image inside you must change, and this takes time. Diligence to do what God's Word says *will* eventually produce the results God said it would.

The reason these things manifested fast for Jesus was because He was highly developed in His faith. It takes longer for some people to receive the manifestation of what they speak because they are not as highly developed in their faith as in their fear.

When I first started applying the Kingdom principles in my life, it took weeks and months before I saw any results with the natural eye.

It took time to change my image about finances. They didn't improve overnight because operating Kingdom principles is a way of life—a process, not a fad!

Operate the Kingdom

Let's summarize what we have learned so far about operating the Kingdom.

In Matthew 12:34-35 Jesus said to the scribes and Pharisees:

O generation of vipers, how can ye, being evil, speak good things? for out of the abundance of the heart the mouth speaketh.

A good man out of the good treasure (or deposit) of the heart bringeth forth good things.

A good man who has stored good treasure—deposited the good Word of God—in his heart will bring forth good things. Many times people pray for *God* to bring forth good things, when actually the Word says *you* must do it.

In Luke 12:32 Jesus said, *Fear not, little flock; for it is your Father's good pleasure to give you the kingdom.* God designed His Kingdom inside you to produce the very thing you need, and Jesus tells how it works. The seed is planted in the heart by speaking it with the mouth. A man speaks the Word of God (the seed) into the heart, or plants it in the soil. Then, as he carries on life as usual, taking no anxious thought, the seed grows up into the thing he needs. It becomes, as Jesus said, *the full corn in the ear.*

You apply the principles of God's Word by being obedient—believe, speak, doubt not, and give. When you do, the Kingdom will produce for you. By sowing God's Word in God's soil (your heart), you will eventually reap a harvest of success.

Things To Remember

Just as it takes time for seed to grow in the soil,
it takes time for you to develop
yourself in Kingdom principles.

Before anything can change on the outside,
your image inside must change—and that takes time.

The more highly developed you are in faith,
the faster the manifestation of what you speak will come.

By diligently applying the principles of the Kingdom,
you will eventually reap a harvest of success!

18

Hope and Faith

Now faith is the substance of things hoped for, the evidence of things not seen.

Hebrews 11:1

Faith is *the substance,* or the raw material, of things you hope for. What do you hope for? Things you desire.

Faith is *the evidence,* or *the proof,* of things not seen. This means you can have proof of the things you can't see.

Hope Is a Goal-Setter

Hope works in the mind. Hope will not produce the thing desired, but it is very important. Many that are sick come to be prayed for because they hope to be healed.

Hope will not heal them, but it will cause them to come for prayer. Hope is really a goal-setter.

Many people have hope in their heart, where faith should be, and faith in their head, where hope should be. Hope works through the intellect. Even though a person is born again, he must renew his mind to the Word of God in order to keep his goals in line with God's goals.

Faith, the substance of things, works out of the heart (the inner man, the spirit man). The heart, which Jesus called the *soil,* will produce the very thing that is planted in it.

Paul wrote, *Be not conformed to this world: but be ye transformed by the renewing of your mind* (Rom. 12:2). He wrote these words to the Roman church, who were born-again. If they needed to renew their minds, so do we.

Hope works out of the head; faith out of the heart. Let me give you an illustration.

A thermostat controls the temperature of your house. In itself, that thermostat has no ability to heat or cool; but when the dial is set at a certain temperature, it sends an impulse, a goal, to the heart of the unit. The unit will work as long as necessary to produce that temperature goal.

If a hermit from the mountains comes to visit you, he will have no understanding of how such a heating unit operates. When he first enters your house, it is hot. He sees you turn the thermostat to 70°, then he feels cool air blowing. In a few minutes, the house is cool.

He asks, "What is that thing?" "A thermostat."

"Where do you get one of them?" "Any hardware store sells them."

As soon as he leaves, he finds a hardware store, buys a thermostat, carries it home, and nails it on his cabin wall.

When the sun comes up the next morning, his cabin gets hot so he turns the thermostat to 60°, sits back, and waits. In a little while, he starts to perspire. Finally he gets up and beats on the thermostat.

"What's wrong with you? Why don't you cool my house?" That thermostat has no substance; it is only a goal-setter. It is like a man that is dealing entirely in the realm of hope. Nothing is connected to the heart of the unit.

Hope has no substance; it is only a goal-setter! There is some power in the mental realm, but it is only a goal-setter! It is the spiritual man—the heart of the unit—that will produce the thing you dial (plant) in it.

Sometimes in the spiritual realm, we try to get faith to work out of the head, when all the head can do is set the goal.

The Bible says faith works in the heart. With the goal-setter in your head, begin to renew your mind to what God said: "Blessed be God! I'm redeemed from the curse of the Law, delivered from the powers of darkness, translated into the Kingdom of the dear Son of God. Because I have given, it is given unto me, good measure, pressed down, shaken together, and running over."

Dial your goal-setter to prosperity and keep it there. It will send an impulse to your heart, the production center.

Release Your Faith

During the winter months, heat is the thing you hope for, and gas is the substance—the raw material—of the heat you hope for.

The raw material for heating your home is connected to the heating unit at all times, but whether or not that raw material is used is another matter. *You* have to turn the dial of the thermostat. When you do, an impulse will be sent to the heart of the unit, a little valve will flip, the pilot light will ignite the gas, and heat will be produced.

The gas, the substance, is there all the time; but until the goal-setter signals the release, it is tied up. This is how some people are with their faith—they have it, but haven't released it.

You must learn to release your faith. Turn the dial of your renewed mind and set it on the goal you want by speaking God's Word concerning that particular area. It will then release the impulse to your heart and produce the desired results.

As you go about your daily activities, speak words of healing and prosperity. Even while you sleep, your heart is working to produce everything you need. Once the thermostat is set, you can rest assured that it will work day and night until it produces what you programmed into it.

If you turn the thermostat to 60°, then up to 90°, then back to 60°, you will probably blow a fuse somewhere. The unit is not designed to function that way. You should set the thermostat at a certain temperature and leave it there.

A Double-minded Man Gets Nothing From God

If any of you lack wisdom, let him ask of God, that giveth to all men liberally, and upbraideth not; and it shall be given him.

But let him ask in faith, nothing wavering. For he that wavereth is like a wave of the sea driven with the wind and tossed.

For let not that man think that he shall receive any thing of the Lord. A double minded man is unstable in all his ways.

James 1:5-8

A double-minded man allows circumstances to influence him and keeps changing his goal. He may set his goal on prosperity; but if somebody tells him, "It's not God's will for you to have riches," he dials back to poverty.

After he goes to an uplifting meeting, he switches his goal to prosperity; but when he goes back to his church and hears, "You're never going to get anything in this life," he turns back to poverty again. He will never become prosperous.

A certain minister tells the story of a paralyzed man who came to one of his meetings in a wheelchair. God healed him, and he walked out of the meeting that night!

The next day his pastor came to see him "to straighten him out." Though the man walked to the door and let him in, the pastor wasn't impressed. He said, "Brother, all healing went out with the apostles. This is of the Devil, and you would be better off in a wheelchair than to be healed this way!"

When the pastor left, the man was unable to move from his chair: He had lost his healing! The goal-setter—the impulse to that man's heart—had been reset for sickness by the words that pastor had spoken.

When he thought, *The pastor may be right. It must be God's will for me to be sick,* he became double-minded and the paralysis came back on him.

Learn the Language of Success

So many times when people pray, they only pray the problem.

"Dear God, I don't know what I'm going to do. I owe all this money! I've lost my job! No money is coming in. Lord, I'll never get these bills paid! This is a big mountain in my life, Lord, and I pray that You'll move it out of the way. Please do something about these problems."

In a prayer like this, the goal is set only on the problem; and as it is prayed, the impulse is released to the heart to produce that goal.

But Jesus said that the Father knows what we have need of, even before we ask Him. (Matt. 6:8.) Our part is to pray the answer.

"Father, in the name of Jesus, Your Word says that whatever I desire, when I pray, believe I receive it and I shall have it. So I am doing that now. I have given, so I believe that it is being given unto me—good measure, pressed down, shaken together, and running over. I proclaim that all my needs are met according to Your riches in glory by Christ Jesus. I can pray this, Father, because it is according to Your Word, and I know that Your Word works!"

When you pray such a prayer as this, there will be people around you who will try to talk you out of it. Don't listen to them. Set your goal on the solution and keep it there!

One lady said she received healing for arthritis after hands were laid on her in the name of Jesus. She was almost totally well for several months. Then people started calling her and leading her into conversations like this:

"How are you doing?" "Oh, I'm just doing fine."

"Well, you know these things come back sometimes. Don't you feel any pain?"

"Well, yes, there is just a little bit." "Yes, that's what I thought."

That lady said she began to listen to that until she eventually lost her healing. When she started talking about her problems, her mind was soon back on the arthritis and it came back on her.

I can never overemphasize the importance of the words you speak. Jesus said that we will have whatsoever we say. (Mark 11:23,24.) We cannot talk sickness and disease and expect to walk in health. The same is true of prosperity. We cannot continue saying things like, "We never can afford the things we need," and expect to walk in prosperity.

It may be true that you can't afford very much at that time, but don't talk about it. Instead, keep your words in line with God's Word: "I have given, so I know it is given unto me. It's mine now even though I don't see it. It belongs to me. God said it is mine, so I am going to believe God!"

God's faith will never fail and God's Word will never fail, but you can cause your own faith to fail by getting your eye on the problem. Learn the language of success and practice it.

The Three D's of Business

1. Don't curse your own fig tree.

Don't speak against your finances, your car, or your business.

2. Don't substitute faith for good business practices.

There is an element of common sense that must be included. Don't forget it.

3. Don't substitute formula for principle.

Don't just speak your desire, but believe what you say will come to pass. Believe *everything* you speak out your mouth will come to pass.

When you believe what you are saying, you are releasing spiritual forces. It won't work just because you say it, but saying it is involved in working the principle.

Do These Things To Make Your Way Prosperous:

Set your goal on prosperity by knowing God's will for your success.

Recognize the Kingdom as the Source of supply.

Seek the Source (Kingdom) instead of things.

Sow good seed in the Kingdom.

Obey God's Word by doing the sayings of Jesus.

Be a giver and not a grabber.

Don't take thought by saying wrong things.

Continue to speak God's Word concerning prosperity.

Begin to apply these principles today. Then you will make your way prosperous and you will have good success.

Things To Remember

Faith is the substance of things hoped for.

Hope has no substance; it is only a goal-setter.

Faith works in the heart; hope works in the head.

The heart produces that which the goal is set on.
Set your goal on the solution, not the problem.

Learn the language of success and practice it.

Dial your goal-setter to prosperity and success,
then keep it there!

19

Prospering or Poormouthing

The world system is a negative stream going its own way to destruction. Many Christians get caught in this negative stream and never seem to recover from the effects of it. One bad thing leads to another. It is like a snowball rolling down a hill; the further it goes, the more destructive it becomes.

The rich man's wealth is his strong city: the destruction of the poor is their poverty.

Proverbs 10:15

Let's examine the lives of two men described in this verse. One we will call Prosperous Joe. He is very positive and bases his actions on the Word of God. The other we will call Poormouth Joe. He is very negative and bases his actions on what he sees, feels, and hears. Both men have good jobs at the same plant.

Prosperous Joe has been confessing abundance and no lack. Several times a day he proclaims, "I have given, and it is given to me; good measure, pressed down, shaken together, and running over do men give unto me."

He has put his faith out for double his salary next year. He says, "I'm giving, but I'll double my giving because I believe I'm going to receive double my salary next year." He is praising God for his prosperity. His favorite Scripture is Proverbs 10:22: *The blessing of the Lord, it maketh rich, and he addeth no sorrow with it.*

In his spare time, Prosperous Joe attends seminars, listens to teaching tapes, and meditates on God's Word.

Poormouth Joe has come from a traditional church which teaches that God leads us "through the fire and through the flood" (then leaves you in the mud!). He has grown up thinking that God brings poverty on you to teach you. His favorite Scripture is 2 Timothy 3:12: *Yea, and all that will live godly in Christ Jesus shall suffer persecution.*

Poormouth Joe is saved and filled with the Holy Ghost, the same as Prosperous Joe. God loves Poormouth Joe just as much as He loves Prosperous Joe. He would do for him what He does for Prosperous Joe if he would operate in the same principles.

While Prosperous Joe is confessing double his salary, Poormouth Joe is always speaking negative things. After he landed a good job at the plant, his wife said, "Glory to God! That's the best job you ever had!" But he only muttered, "Yeah, but I'll probably be the first one laid off! You watch and see! Nothing will ever last for me."

Because of their new income, his wife talked to him about buying a new car. His response was, "As sure as we buy that car, I'll lose my job!"

Without even realizing it, he is bringing negative things on himself through his words.

Almost every night after watching the news, Poormouth Joe tells his wife, "This recession is really bad, and people are being laid off. I'll probably be the first one to go at our plant."

One morning he goes to work, and his fear has come upon him. The boss says, "We are cutting back and we don't need you anymore." So Poormouth Joe goes home to have a pity party. He says, "Oh, Lord, I knew it was going to happen! I told my wife three months ago that this was going to happen!"

Together, he and his wife cry half the night. They even call the neighbors who cry with them and give them a load of sympathy—but no Word.

Prosperous Joe, who has been confessing double his salary, goes to work that same morning and gets laid off also; but he knows what Jesus said: "If a man will do My sayings, he won't be shaken when the negative stream beats against him."

Prosperous Joe says, "Glory to God! I still believe I will double my salary this year. This may not be the place where I'll do it, but I will, for I believe I receive."

When he gets home, his wife says, "What are you doing home so early?"

"I lost my job, honey; but, praise God, I'll get a better one. This is our chance to prove that God's Word works. Get the Bible and let's confess what God's Word says about this situation." (Luke 6:47,48.)

That night, after confessing the Word of God, Prosperous Joe sleeps well. He finds that the Word of God has not changed, even though he has lost his job. But because

Poormouth Joe had a pity party all night, crying, "Why me, Lord?" it's early in the morning before he gets to sleep. Wallowing in misery feels good to his flesh. He believes that somehow God is getting glory out of his suffering.

Prosperous Joe's spirit is filled with good words: "Blessed be God! Whatever I do will prosper. No weapon formed against me will prosper. I expect this situation to bless me!" Proverbs 10:15 describes Prosperous Joe: *The rich man's wealth is his strong city,* and God's Word is his wealth.

Prosperous Joe has sown good seed into his spirit and has set his goal on prosperity. While he sleeps, his spirit searches the avenues of God's wisdom. It takes several nights, but his spirit finds a way to bring to pass the things he has spoken in faith.

Both men are operating the same principle of seedtime and harvest—one positive, the other negative.

Notice the type of seed Poormouth Joe plants in his spirit: "I'll probably be the first one laid off." After he loses his job, he plants another seed by telling his wife: *"We'll probably lose our house.* The note is due in January. How can I pay it? We're going to lose the house just as sure as the world. You watch and see what I tell you."

Proverbs 10:15 says the poor man's poverty is his destruction. This perfectly describes Poormouth Joe. He just continues to become more and more negative as the circumstances worsen.

One morning Prosperous Joe says, "I feel impressed in my spirit to go downtown and look for work."

The very same morning, Poormouth Joe gets an impression: "I need to go downtown this morning."

So both of them start downtown.

As Prosperous Joe is driving down the boulevard, he is impressed in his spirit to have a cup of coffee; so at 9:00 A.M. he drives into the parking lot of a local restaurant, goes in, and sits in the second booth. At 9:03 A.M. Joe Blow, an old school buddy, walks in. They greet each other.

"Well, Prosperous Joe, how are you doing?"

"Just great, Joe."

"You know, you have been on my mind for several days. What are you doing now?"

"I was working at the plant until a few days ago when I got laid off; but, thank God, I'm going to get a better job!"

Joe Blow says, "That's amazing! I am building a manufacturing plant in town, and I need a manager. You are exactly what I need. When I was praying the other day, your name came to me, but I had no idea where you were."

This meeting was no accident. Joe Blow hires Prosperous Joe at twice the salary he was making previously. Prosperous Joe's spirit produced exactly what he had spoken! *A man shall be satisfied with good by the fruit of his mouth: and the recompence of a man's hands shall be rendered unto him* (Prov. 12:14).

As Poormouth Joe is driving down the same boulevard, he is having a pity party, thinking, *How am I ever going to get out of this mess? Why do these things always seem to happen to me?*

Suddenly, he gets the desire for a cup of coffee. Instead of pulling into the parking lot of the restaurant where Prosperous Joe is, he drives to another restaurant down the street.

Joe Blow was looking for two men and would have hired Poormouth Joe if he had walked in, but Poormouth Joe had deceived his heart with his words: *We will lose our house. I'll never find a good job again.* He set the goal and his human spirit led him to what he said. He was led by his spirit to the wrong place for coffee because the seed was wrong.

A wholesome tongue is a tree of life: but perverseness therein is a breach in the spirit.

Proverbs 15:4

While Prosperous Joe's spirit had been searching the avenues of God's wisdom all night long to find how to get him in a place to double his salary, Poormouth Joe's spirit had been searching all night to find out how he could lose his car and his house. The question he posed for his spirit to answer was not, "How will I prosper?" but *How will I fail?* The seed is planted and, in searching for a way to get him exactly what he had been saying, Poormouth Joe's spirit found a way to keep him from the restaurant where the good deals were.

Then as the waitress is bringing coffee to Poormouth Joe, she trips and pours it all over him! His day is ruined. It was his only clean suit, so he returns home to have another pity party.

The next morning when he hears about Prosperous Joe, Poormouth Joe complains, "He's the luckiest guy who ever lived! I don't understand why God blesses him but won't bless me. Nothing good ever happens to me."

...the destruction of the poor is their poverty.

Proverbs 10:15

Later while he is shaving, he gets another impression: "I heard that the plant in the next town is hiring now. I feel led to go over there."

His spirit is leading him there because it is working to bring him what he has been saying. Good, bad, or indifferent, the outcome depends on the seed that was sown.

Following his impression, Poormouth Joe goes to the next town and gets a job at that plant. His spirit led him to one of the few places in the nation where he could get a job and then lose it in thirty days! A month after he starts, the plant goes bankrupt and lays off all the help.

By January his harvest has come: He loses his car and his house. Still, he can't understand it: *Why did God allow this to happen to me?*

God wanted to bless Poormouth Joe in the same way He blessed Prosperous Joe because He loves both of them the same; but so many of God's people are destroyed for lack of knowledge.

Yes, this was a hypothetical situation, but it has been true in the lives of so many of God's people.

God wants you to take hold of His principles and be a Prosperous Joe. It is the law of seedtime and harvest. Start sowing your crop today!

I believe the words of the Apostle Paul make a very fitting close to this story:

And the servant of the Lord must not strive; but be gentle unto all men, apt to teach, patient,

In meekness instructing those that oppose themselves; if God peradventure will give them repentance to the acknowledging of the truth;

And that they may recover themselves out of the snare of the devil, who are taken captive by him at his will.

2 Timothy 2:24-26

You must recover yourself out of the negative stream. No one can do it for you. **The first step to recovery is to recognize where you are and have a desire to recover.**

...when the desire cometh, it is a tree of life.

Proverbs 13:12

Prayer of Salvation

God loves you—no matter who you are, no matter what your past. God loves you so much that He gave His one and only begotten Son for you. The Bible tells us that "…whoever believes in him shall not perish but have eternal life" (John 3:16 NIV). Jesus laid down His life and rose again so that we could spend eternity with Him in heaven and experience His absolute best on earth. If you would like to receive Jesus into your life, say the following prayer out loud and mean it from your heart.

Heavenly Father, I come to You admitting that I am a sinner. Right now, I choose to turn away from sin, and I ask You to cleanse me of all unrighteousness. I believe that Your Son, Jesus, died on the cross to take away my sins. I also believe that He rose again from the dead so that I might be forgiven of my sins and made righteous through faith in Him. I call upon the name of Jesus Christ to be the Savior and Lord of my life. Jesus, I choose to follow You and ask that You fill me with the power of the Holy Spirit. I declare that right now I am a child of God. I am free from sin and full of the righteousness of God. I am saved in Jesus' name. Amen.

Charles Capps is a former farmer and land developer who travels throughout the United States, teaching and preaching the truths of God's Word. He shares from practical, firsthand experience how Christians can apply the Word to the circumstances of life and live victoriously.

In the mid '90's the Lord gave Charles an assignment to teach end-time events and a revelation of the coming of the Lord.

Besides authoring several books, including the best selling *The Tongue, A Creative Force*, and the mini-book series *God's Creative Power*®, which has sold over 4 million copies, Charles also has a nationwide daily radio ministry and weekly TV broadcast called "Concepts of Faith."

Charles and his wife, Peggy, make their home in England, Arkansas. Both their daughters, Annette and Beverly, are involved in full-time ministry.

For a free brochure of CDs, DVDs and books
by Charles Capps, write:
Charles Capps Ministries
Box 69
England, AR 72046
www.charlescapps.com
1-877-396-9400

Powerful Teaching From Charles Capps

You can find more dynamic teaching from Charles Capps in these revolutionary books.

Your Spiritual Authority

Charles Capps shares a penetrating message on the believer's legal right to exercise authority in the earth today. This delegated authority was given to every Christian so that the sick can be healed, finances can be loosed, and those bound by Satan may be free. You will learn that you have dominion through your words, that your body gives you authority on the earth that being born of the Spirit gives you the ability to use Jesus' name, and many other powerful principles.

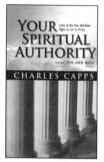

ISBN: 978-0-9820320-4-6

Releasing the Ability of God Through Prayer

God's Word is alive and powerful! It is living substance. When you learn to pray in line with God's Word, you release the ability of God and bring Him on the scene in your behalf. Discover the power of prayer that is governed by spiritual laws and designed to work for you. It is more powerful than the laws of nature that rule the universe today.

ISBN: 978-0-9820320-2-2

Available at fine bookstores everywhere

Speak Life and Live Better, Stronger and Longer!

Join the millions whose lives have been changed by the *God's Creative Power® Series*. This dynamic series from Charles Capps has sold over 5 million copies. Each book reveals powerful teaching on the power of your words and includes scriptural confessions that will change the way you think and the way you live.

God's Creative Power® Will Work for You—
Over 4 Million Sold!

Charles Capps' original mini-book reveals that the power of the spoken word can change your destiny. God created the universe by speaking it into existence. He has given the same ability to you through your words. To be effective in life, you must speak words of faith. Let faith-filled words put you over!
(Also available in Spanish)

ISBN: 978-0-9820320-6-0

God's Creative Power® for Healing—
Over 1.5 Million Sold!

This powerful book combines all new teaching with Scripture confessions for healing. You will learn how you can release the ability of God for your healing with the words of your mouth.
(Also available in Spanish)

ISBN: 978-0-9820320-0-8

God's Creative Power® for Finances—
the newest release!
By Charles Capps and Annette Capps

Words are the most powerful things in the universe today. They can make the difference in your finances and your wellbeing. Learn to turn your financial situation around by following the powerful principles of faith contained in this book.

ISBN: 978-0-9820320-1-5

The God's Creative Power® Gift Collection By Charles Capps and Annette Capps is now available and includes all three books in beautiful Italian leather. A perfect gift for any occasion for you and your loved ones! (Also available in Spanish)

ISBN: 978-0-9820320-3-9

Available at fine bookstores everywhere

Books by Charles Capps

The Tongue — A Creative Force

Changing the Seen and Shaping the Unseen

Faith That Will Not Change

Faith and Confession

Faith That Will Work for You

When Jesus Prays Through You

The Messenger of Satan

God's Creative Power® for Healing
(Also Available in Spanish)

God's Creative Power® Will Work for You
(Also Available in Spanish)

End Time Events

God's Image of You

Seedtime and Harvest
(Also Available in Spanish)

Hope — A Partner to Faith
(Also Available in Spanish)

How You Can Avoid Tragedy

Kicking Over Sacred Cows

The Substance of Things

The Light of Life in the Spirit of Man

Books by Charles Capps and Annette Capps

Angels

God's Creative Power® for Finances

God's Creative Power® Gift Collection
(Also Available in Spanish)

Books by Annette Capps

Quantum Faith

Reverse the Curse in Your Body and Emotions

Understanding the Persecution